Art, Trade, and Cultural Mediation in Asia, 1600–1950

Raquel A. G. Reyes
Editor

Art, Trade, and Cultural Mediation in Asia, 1600–1950

Editor
Raquel A. G. Reyes
Department of History
School of Oriental and African Studies
London, UK

ISBN 978-1-137-57236-3   ISBN 978-1-137-57237-0 (eBook)
https://doi.org/10.1057/978-1-137-57237-0

Library of Congress Control Number: 2018957683

© The Editor(s) (if applicable) and The Author(s) 2019
The author(s) has/have asserted their right(s) to be identified as the author(s) of this work in accordance with the Copyright, Designs and Patents Act 1988.
This work is subject to copyright. All rights are solely and exclusively licensed by the Publisher, whether the whole or part of the material is concerned, specifically the rights of translation, reprinting, reuse of illustrations, recitation, broadcasting, reproduction on microfilms or in any other physical way, and transmission or information storage and retrieval, electronic adaptation, computer software, or by similar or dissimilar methodology now known or hereafter developed.
The use of general descriptive names, registered names, trademarks, service marks, etc. in this publication does not imply, even in the absence of a specific statement, that such names are exempt from the relevant protective laws and regulations and therefore free for general use.
The publisher, the authors and the editors are safe to assume that the advice and information in this book are believed to be true and accurate at the date of publication. Neither the publisher nor the authors or the editors give a warranty, express or implied, with respect to the material contained herein or for any errors or omissions that may have been made. The publisher remains neutral with regard to jurisdictional claims in published maps and institutional affiliations.

Cover illustration: © Melisa Hasan

This Palgrave Pivot imprint is published by the registered company Springer Nature Limited
The registered company address is: The Campus, 4 Crinan Street, London, N1 9XW, United Kingdom

For Gaia Tera Vida Reyes

ACKNOWLEDGEMENTS

This book was inspired by a chance meeting with Thomas DaCosta Kaufmann and Michael North at the Netherlands Institute for Advanced Studies (NIAS) in Wassenaar, where they and I were both fellows in 2010. We continued talking and sharing ideas at the International Convention for Asian Scholars (ICAS) in Hawai'i in the following year. After trips to the Philippines to look at church architecture, and to Jakarta to visit VOC landmarks, the book started to materialize. I warmly thank the contributors to this book for their friendship and faith in me over the years; Benito J. Legarda, Jnr and Jim Richardson for their encouragement and constructive comments; and the editors at Palgrave Pivot who worked closely with me every step of the way.

Amsterdam, The Netherlands   Raquel A. G. Reyes
London, UK

Contents

Introduction Raquel A. G. Reyes	1
Japanese Export Lacquer and Global Art History: An Art of Mediation in Circulation Thomas DaCosta Kaufmann	13
Paradise in Stone: Representations of New World Plants and Animals on Spanish Colonial Churches in the Philippines Raquel A. G. Reyes	43
Betel, Tobacco and Beverages in Southeast Asia William Gervase Clarence-Smith	75
Domestic Interiors in Seventeenth- and Eighteenth-Century Batavia Michael North	103
Index	123

NOTES ON CONTRIBUTORS

William Gervase Clarence-Smith is Professor of the Economic History of Asia and Africa at the School of Oriental and African Studies (SOAS), University of London. His research interests include the History of tropical beverages, masticatories, livestock, and textiles; Middle Eastern diasporas; religion, slavery and sexual norms with special reference to Southeast Asia. He is the author of *The Economics of the Indian Ocean Slave Trade in the Nineteenth Century* (Reprint of 1989 edition; Abingdon and New York: Routledge, 2015); *Islam and the Abolition of Slavery* (London: Hurst & Company, 2006); and *Cocoa and Chocolate 1765–1914* (Routledge, 2000).

Thomas DaCosta Kaufmann is Frederick Marquand Professor of Art and Archaeology at the University of Princeton. He teaches and publishes on European art and architecture 1500–1800 in its global context, the theory and practice of world art history, and the geography and historiography of art. He has been a fellow of the American Academy in Rome and the American Academy in Berlin and is a member of the Royal Flemish, Polish, and Swedish Academies of Science. He is the author of several books including *Arcimboldo: Visual Jokes, Natural History and Still-Life Painting* (University of Chicago Press, 2009) and co-editor of *Mediating Netherlandish Art and Material Culture in Asia* (Amsterdam University Press and University of Chicago Press, 2014).

Michael North is Chair of Modern History at the University of Greifswald. He is a specialist in monetary and financial history and of the history of commerce and culture. In 2010–2011, he held the Fulbright Distinguished Chair in Modern German Studies at the University of California at Santa Barbara. He is the author of several books including *Material Delight and the Joy of Living: Cultural Consumption in Germany in the Age of Enlightenment* (Aldershot, 2008), *Artistic and Cultural Exchanges Between Europe and Asia, 1400–1900* (Surrey, 2010).

Raquel A. G. Reyes is an associate research fellow at the School of Oriental and African Studies, University of London, and former British Academy post-doctoral fellow in London. She works on the history of science and medicine, history of gender and sexuality, global trade and local cultural innovation in early modern Southeast Asia, with particular reference to the Philippines. She is the author of *Love, Passion and Patriotism: Sexuality and the Philippine Propaganda Movement* (University of Washington Press and NUS Press, 2008) and co-editor of *Sexual Diversity in Asia c.600–1950* (Routledge, 2012). She is also a columnist for the Manila Times.

LIST OF FIGURES

Introduction
Fig. 1   Virgin and Christ Child exhibited in The Victoria and Albert Museum, London (Photo by Author)   2

Japanese Export Lacquer and Global Art History: An Art of Mediation in Circulation
Fig. 1   Pyx for Communion Hosts, Japan, Momoyama Period, late sixteenth century, black lacquered cryptomeria wood decorated with gold and silver power and inlaid with mother-of-pearl, Lisbon, Museo de Arte Antiga, inv. 18 cx © Lisbon, Museo de Arte Antiga, Direção-Geral do Património Cultural/Arquivo de Documentação Fotográfica (DGPC/ADF)   19
Fig. 2   Portuguese escaping from a mined building at Hoogly, detail of *The Capture of Port Hoogly*, c. 1634, Padshanameh, Royal Library, Windsor Castle, fol. 117r, RCIN 1005025 Royal Collection Trust/© Her Majesty Queen Elizabeth II 2018   29
Fig. 3   Tray (*Batea*) Mexico, seventeenth century. Lacquered wood with inlaid lacquer decoration, diameter 12 5/16 in. (56.7 cm) Hispanic Society of America LS1978   35

Paradise in Stone: Representations of New World Plants and Animals on Spanish Colonial Churches in the Philippines
Fig. 1   Pan-ay Church, pineapple-shaped finials (Photo by Author)   53
Fig. 2   Paete Church, detail showing St James on horse-back (Photo by Author)   56

Fig. 3   Miag-ao Church, pediment (Photo by Author)   63
Fig. 4   Miag-ao Church, pediment detail (Photo by Author)   63
Fig. 5   San Joaquin Church, pediment detail (Photo by Author)   64

LIST OF TABLES

Domestic Interiors in Seventeenth- and Eighteenth-Century Batavia
Table 1   Sample of Chinese inventories in Batavia with works
          of art (Compiled by the Author)   110
Table 2   Sample of Batavia inventories of non-Dutch, non-Chinese
          inhabitants (Compiled by the Author)   112

Introduction

Raquel A. G. Reyes

Abstract Recent years have seen a surge of interest in early modern global trade and the kinds of interactions and exchanges that arose between Asia and Europe as a consequence. However, sometimes these investigations have tended to lose sight of the more quotidian diffusion of trade goods and objects and their impact on local communities, of the role played by the host of intermediaries who facilitated the process (such as apothecaries, artisans, missioner priests), and of the small but significant changes wrought on aspects of everyday life and sensibilities.

Keywords Europe · Asia · Trans-Pacific · Intermediaries · Global trade

In the Sculpture Room of London's Victoria and Albert Museum (The V&A), there is a small, exquisitely carved ivory statuette called the *Virgin and the Christ Child*. It was made, in all likelihood, in Manila by Chinese or Filipino sculptors, sometime in the eighteenth century or possibly earlier (Fig. 1). Both the Virgin and her Child have unmistakably oriental features, with heavy lidded eyes and full lips. Their striated hair retains traces of gilding, and on their lips and eyes are remnants of

R. A. G. Reyes (✉)
School of Oriental and African Studies, University of London, London, UK

© The Author(s) 2019
R. A. G. Reyes (ed.), *Art, Trade, and Cultural Mediation in Asia, 1600–1950*, https://doi.org/10.1057/978-1-137-57237-0_1

Fig. 1 Virgin and Christ Child exhibited in The Victoria and Albert Museum, London (Photo by Author)

red and brown pigment suggesting that they were once richly colored. The Virgin's face is serene, and there is a hint of a smile. The Christ Child is naked, plump and playful. He tugs at his mother's headdress with his right hand while mischievously kicks up his right leg.

The Virgin's robe is a masterpiece of fine carving. It cascades in long, sensuous, liquid folds, and pools around her feet which remain hidden beneath the extravagant drapery. A portion of her blouse peels away to reveal a single bare breast. At the back, there is a distinctive little fold or tuck in her dress, an idiosyncratic detail common to Madonna figurines made in the Philippines.[1] It is a sophisticated carving, executed by a skilled and confident hand.

From the late sixteenth century onward, the port city of Manila was the hub of a galleon trade that was a magnet for anyone mercantile minded. The galleons, monumental ships heavily laden with luxury goods and treasures, from silks and spices, to porcelain and jewelry, would sail yearly from Manila across the Pacific to Acapulco on the west coast of Mexico, where the goods would be paid for in silver, mined from the conquered lands of South America, that was demanded by the Chinese.

Manila was the epicenter of fine craft-work wrought in luxurious and costly materials, including ivory. Raw ivory from elephants' tusks was sumptuous and exotic. It was imported into the Philippines from various sources: From Africa via the slender waterway connecting the Persian Gulf to the Arabian Sea, and from Cambodia and Thailand.[2]

Chinese artisans flocked to Manila and settled in an enclave specifically designated for the Chinese population called the Parián, a name derived from the markets in Mexico City. Known as *sangleyes*, these non-Christian traders and craftsmen constituted the largest Chinese trading community outside of mainland China.[3] Craftsmen were presented with a ready market. Ivories of sacred and divine subjects that adhered to Christian themes and the Catholic faith were hugely popular export items. In the Parián, there was a more or less organized and efficient

---

[1] Marjorie Trusted, "Survivors of a Shipwreck: Ivories from a Manila Galleon of 1601," *Hispanic Research Journal* 14, no. 5 (October 2013): 446–62.

[2] Ibid.

[3] Lourdes Diaz-Trechuelo, "The Role of the Chinese in the Philippine Domestic Economy (1570–1770)," in *The Chinese in the Philippines 1570–1770, Vol. 1*, ed. Alfonso Felix (Manila: Solidaridad, 1966), 175–210.

production line that repeatedly churned out the same images in large quantities without, it seems, compromising on quality. Such was the constant demand for these items that production expanded. Workshops were set up by the Christianized Chinese communities north of the Pasig River, in Binondo and Tondo, and overseen by the Dominicans and Augustinians. These workshops specialized in the production of ivory sculpture (crucifixes, statues of saints, the infant Christ and the Madonna), and also paintings and altarpieces, for the local market and for export to Macau, Latin America, and Europe. The first bishop of Manila, a Dominican friar, paid fulsome praise, declaring the carvings made by the *sangleyes* to be better than those from Flanders.[4]

The assembled figures were very popular—diminutive in size and often produced in sets, they might be placed in a domestic oratory, or in a small, unconsecrated chapel or niche where priests could say mass for the household, or as part of a small *retablo* kept in the bedroom for personal and private prayer. Manila's ivory carvers, along with Indian ivory carvers from Goa, also made high quality parts—heads, hands, and feet, designed to be attached to a wooden armature for dressing, called the *imagen de vestir*, or joined to bodies made from wood carved either in the Philippines, Goa, or Latin America. Gilding, imitative of Chinese silk garments, often decorated the polychrome wood. The production of parts was a significant industry and amounted to a form of 'global outsourcing'. The brilliance of these carvers, notes Gauvin Bailey Alexander, lies in "the way they imparted indigenous styles to Western prototypes, which were derived mostly from Antwerp prints".[5]

The manufacture of religious images served several purposes. Small-scale figures were produced for the friar and missionary orders—the

---

[4] Regalado Trota Jose and Ramon N. Villegas, *Power + Faith + Image: Philippine Art in Ivory from the 16th to the 19th Century* (Makati: Ayala Foundation, 2004); Margareta Mercedes and Estella Marcos, *Ivories from the Far Eastern Provinces of Spain and Portugal* (Monterrey: Espejo de Obsidiana Ediciones, 1997); and Gauvin Alexander Bailey, "Translation and Metamorphosis in the Catholic Ivories of China, Japan, and the Philippines, 1561–1800," in *Ivories of the Portuguese Empire*, ed. Gauvin Alexander Bailey, Michel Massing, and Nuno Vassallo e Silva (Lisbon: Scribe, 2013).

[5] Gauvin Alexander Bailey, "Religious Orders and the Arts of Asia," in *Made in the Americas: The New World Discovers Asia*, ed. Dennis Carr (Boston: Museum of Fine Arts, 2015), 94–95. Elsewhere, Bailey has called the hybridized works of art and architecture which emerged in the Iberian empires in Asia and Africa as "acculturative art". See Gauvin Alexander Bailey, *Art of Colonial Latin America* (London: Phaidon Press, 2005), 367.

Augustinians, Dominicans, Franciscans, and Jesuits—who pursued commerce and religious conversion with equal fervor. Missionaries depended upon the commercial trade of the Manila galleons for the Asian objects that found their way into Latin America, and they invested in this trade that helped support their missionary activities. These figures were effective evangelical aids. As devotional objects, they aided in the conversion and instruction of people in the new faith. A Jesuit priest traveling to New Spain via Guam is known to have brought with him a Philippine-made sculpture of the Virgin Immaculate, as did a Franciscan friar who transported an eighteenth century ivory version to a monastery in Santiago; while a Philippine-made ivory crucifix was carried by a Jesuit missionary on the Chiquitos missions of lowland Bolivia.[6] Second, ivory objects were important to a flourishing collectors' market. Aristocrats and elites in Spain, Portugal, Italy, the German-speaking lands, and elsewhere in Europe, admired and valued the precious and rare ivory itself which were sought out as prized additions to collections of exotica, curiosity cabinets and cabinets of wonder.[7] Moreover, the enthusiasm for Asian artifacts frequently went hand in hand with the interest in Asian antiquity and culture among intellectuals and natural philosophers in Europe.[8]

Religious ivory sculpture such as the *Virgin and Christ Child* is illustrative of the patterns and processes of cultural mediation with which this book is concerned. Through trade, Europeans and Asians transported the raw materials from which the luxury object was created. Europeans conveyed the design, motif, and function of the object to local producers, Chinese and Filipinos. These artisans brought with them their own labor practices and worked under the influence or intervention from European Catholic clerics, assimilating, adapting, and imitating designs and motifs, as well as incorporating their own Asian aesthetics. With the involvement of Europeans, the objects then traveled to other parts

---

[6] Bailey, "Religious Orders and the Arts of Asia," 94.

[7] Just two spectacular examples being the princely collections of the Medici in Florence, and the Habsburg *kunstkammern* in Prague. On the mania for collecting 'indian' artifacts, see Jessica Keating and Lia Markey, "'Indian' Objects in Medici and Austrian-Habsburg Inventories: A Case-Study of the Sixteenth Century Term," *Journal of History of Collections* 23, no. 2 (2011): 283–300.

[8] R. J. W. Evans and A. Marr, eds., *Curiosity and Wonder from the Renaissance to the Enlightenment* (Aldershot, 2006).

of Asia, to Europe and to the Americas. Cultural mediation is thus here construed as the many and varied processes of exchange, artistic practices and transfer of techniques, of the role colonial art played in global trade, making money and religious conversion, and the role of intermediaries, transporting, distributing and circulating art objects around the globe.

Commercial and cultural exchanges between Europeans and Asians, or broadly between 'East and West', have long enjoyed scholarly attention and have been the subject of a number of major museum exhibitions.[9] More recently however, scholars have begun to question the 'European-Asian' rubric, which is increasingly being seen as far too narrow and confining. Noting the ascendance of a 'global turn' in art history, Kristina Kleutghen has explored how trade, exploration, and diplomacy brought about artistic exchange across East Asia, Southeast Asia, around India, the Indian Ocean to the Middle East.[10] Forging a new transpacific field of investigation, Dana Leibsohn and Meha Priyadarshini have suggested viewing the transpacific "not as the distance between Acapulco and Manila but as a construct of multiple geographies."[11] In *Circulations in the Global History of Art*, Thomas DaCosta Kaufmann and his co-editors have questioned diffusionist, vertical and hierarchical narratives of art history that have tended to treat objects and cultural relations along such binary and essentialist lines as 'Western and non-Western' or 'center-periphery'. Artifacts such as Asian and American lacquer ware and even the Japanese *fumi-e*, a flat image carved from stone or wooden blocks that depicted the Virgin Mary and

---

[9] *A Special Exhibition—The History of Cultural Exchange Between East and West in the 16th and 17th Century—The Galleon Trade and the VOC* (Tokyo: Tobacco and Salt Museum, 1998); Dennis Carr, et al., *Made in the Americas: The New World Discovers Asia* (Boston: Museum of Fine Arts, 2015); Michael North, ed., *Artistic and Cultural Exchanges Between Europe and Asia, 1400–1900: Rethinking Markets, Workshops and Collections* (Farnham: Ashgate, 2010).

[10] Kristina Kleutghen, ed, "Explorations of Intra-Asian Artistic Exchange," *Journal 18 East-Southeast*, no. 4 (Fall 2017) (published online); See also the respective essays by Tom Hoogervorst, "Tracing Maritime Connections Between Island Southeast Asia and the Indian Ocean World," and John Miksic, "Spheres of Ceramic Exchange in Southeast Asia, Ninth to Sixteenth Centuries," in *The Routledge Handbook of Archaeology and Globalization*, ed. Tamar Hodos (London: Routledge, 2016).

[11] Dana Leibsohn and Meha Priyadarshini, "Transpacific: Beyond Silk and Silver," *Colonial Latin American Review* 25, no. 1: 1–15, https://doi.org/10.1080/10609164.2016.1180780.

Christ and was designed to be stepped on, were trade luxury items transported by the Manila Galleon trade and the Dutch East India Company, the VOC. But their markets, material and historical contexts, processes of mediation, and conditions of cultural transfer were hitherto left unexplored in orthodox narratives of these global enterprises. The authors argue for a more transnational, globalized, and historically materialist approach to the study of art objects, artistic expressions and artistic consumption: 'By "material conditions" we mean not only the materiality of the object and the image, but also the diverse modes of circulation and the various contexts in which they occur...attention to these conditions is a requisite for describing and understanding artistic circulations.'[12]

In chapter "Japanese Export Lacquer and Global Art History: An Art of Mediation in Circulation" of this book, Thomas DaCosta Kaufmann contemplates a single luxury object—Japanese lacquer ware—and traces its production, its material composition, the techniques of its manufacture, and its circulation, through processes of cultural mediation in which the European role might be seen as an insertion in a long and complex chain of circumstances, interactions, and encounters. As Kaufmann discusses, the lacquer material utilized to produce objects manufactured in Japan was likely to have been extracted from Southeast Asian trees growing in Myanmar, Burma, Thailand, or Cambodia, and brought to Japan on VOC ships. As gifts and highly sought after export goods, Japanese lacquer ware was presented to European governments by Southeast Asian diplomats, transported to Macau, Malacca, Goa, via Africa and Lisbon on Portuguese ships, or became part of the precious cargo carried by Spanish galleons that left Manila for New Spain and onto Europe.

The Manila Galleon trade was key to what Serge Gruzinski has termed 'an Iberian worldwide diffusion.' Since the publication of William Lytle Schurz's pioneering study on the Manila galleons and Trans-Pacific commerce in 1939, a rich corpus of work has emerged that has closely examined diverse aspects of the galleon trade's global reach: From the origins of the galleon trade in relation to Spanish expansion, the profitability of transpacific commerce, the demand and supply factors that gave impetus to the trade, and, more recently, the political complexities that

---

[12] Thomas DaCosta Kaufmann, Catherine Dossin, and Beatrice Joyeux-Prunel, eds., *Circulations in the Global History of Art* (Burlington, VT: Ashgate, 2015), 3.

enmeshed the economies of China, Japan, and Spain in the Philippines.[13] These new revisionist histories make clear that the trade was immense, that indeed it was capable of financially bolstering the Spanish empire, and that its economic success continued well after the initial spectacular commercial boom of the late sixteenth and early seventeenth century.[14]

'Re-dimensioned on the planetary scale' writes Gruzinski, there occurred, from the late fifteenth century onward, an unprecedented moment in history that was witness to what he has grandly termed the 'planetarization' of Christianization and Westernization.[15] Under the 'impulse' of personnel from Spain and Portugal—soldiers, sailors, missionaries traders, civil officials, connections were made that tied 'the four corners of the globe.' Economic and social organizations, government and bureaucratic structures, as well as intellectual and artistic exchanges were tremendously and directly affected by this planetary process: 'The literary, visual, and musical expressions of Iberian domination attest to the successful diffusion of an art, mannerism, which blossomed on several continents simultaneously.'[16]

Material interactions arising from the Galleon trade and the cultural and commercial exchanges it facilitated, is discussed by Reyes in chapter "Paradise in Stone: Representations of New World Plants and Animals on Spanish Colonial Churches in the Philippines" in relation to Spanish colonial church architecture in the Philippines. Churches in the southern Luzon and Visayas regions of the Philippines displayed fabulously

---

[13] Most recent works are Birgit Tremml-Werner, *Spain, China, and Japan in Manila, 1571–1644: Local Comparisons, Global Connections* (Amsterdam University Press, 2015); Arturo Giraldez, *The Age of Trade: The Manila Galleons and the Dawn of the Global Economy* (London: Rowman and Littlefield, 2015). Also selected essays in *A Primera Viagem Histórica da Globalização* in *Revista de Cultura*, International Edition 17, January 2006 (Instituto Cultural de Macao).

[14] Dennis O. Flynn, Lionel Frost, and A. J. H. Latham, "Introduction," in *Pacific Centuries: Pacific and Pacific Rim History Since the Sixteenth Century* (London and New York: Routledge, 1999), xxxiii.

[15] Serge Gruzinski, "Art History and Iberian Worldwide Diffusion: Westernization/Globalization/Americanization," in *Circulations in the Global History of Art*, ed. Thomas DaCosta Kaufmann, Catherine Dossin, and Beatrice Joyeux-Prunel (Surrey: Ashgate, 2015), 48–49.

[16] Ibid.

elaborate facades. Taking a historical materialist approach,[17] Reyes focuses in particular on artistic depictions of New World flora and fauna, enquiring into the influence of certain material conditions, such as geographic location, connections to trading networks and local industries, the availability of local labor and materials, the impact of American edible plants on local diets, and the religious-didactic purposes of the designs. Executed by Chinese and Filipino stonemasons, under the guidance and supervision of European priests, the facades manifested a convergence and cultural syncretism of local, Chinese, American, Muslim, and European influences and adaptations. Reyes interrogates and problematizes the concept of 'Filipino style,' and attempts to discern elements of church architecture that might be seen as evidence of indigenous agency.

In the early modern period, every major European power nursed the grandiose, but simple ambition to secure all-important sea routes to the spices, silks, and other riches of the East. Ownership of the Moluccas, better known as the Spice Islands, and control of the trade in cinnamon, cloves, nutmeg and pepper, that is—the spice trade—then the most lucrative trade in the world, figured centrally in dreams of an empire in the Pacific and motivated extraordinary voyages, from Christopher Columbus (1451–1506) to Vasco da Gama (1469–1524). Spain had lost her crucial claim to the Moluccas and the spice trade to Portugal in 1529, but gained a foothold in the Pacific by colonizing the Philippine archipelago and, thanks to the ingenuity of the circumnavigator and Augustinian friar Andrés de Urdaneta (1498–1568), had discovered a fast and efficient return route across the Pacific to Mexico, a factor critical to the commercial success of the Spanish colonial enterprise in the Pacific.

Yet, arguably, it was the Dutch who came closest to realizing the dream of global trading dominance. Soon after their arrival in the Indonesian archipelago around 1600, they wrested control of the Moluccas from the Portuguese; a couple of years later created the formidable the VOC;

---

[17] Ramón Gutiérrez and Graciela María Viñuales, "The Artistic and Architectural Legacy of the Jesuits in Spanish America" and Gauvin Alexander Bailey, "Jesuit Art and Architecture in Asia," in *The Jesuits and the Arts 1540–1773*, ed. John W. O'Malley, S. J. Harris, and Gauvin Alexander Bailey (Philadelphia, St. Joseph's University Press, 2005), 311–61.

turned the port city of Jayakerta on western Java, into the capital city of Batavia and the main Asian headquarters of the VOC, established trading arrangements with the Japanese on the artificial island of Deshima, in the port of Nagasaki in Japan, and through ruthless 'total war' campaigns, enforced a trade monopoly on nutmeg, cloves, and mace on the Spice Islands, in addition to securing much of the trade in pepper and cinnamon. At their zenith, VOC territories and trading posts stretched between the Cape of Good Hope and Japan, and six million pounds of black pepper were being annually imported to the Netherlands.[18]

The importation of luxury goods from Asia, particularly porcelain, by the VOC and how this influenced taste in Europe is well documented. In *Mediating Netherlandish Art and Material Culture in Asia*, Thomas DaCosta Kaufmann and Michael North discuss the roles played by the VOC and the various local agents within and outside the European trading companies, in the production and reception of Dutch art in colonial societies in Asia. The mediation of Netherlandish art, they argue, much depended on the local social and ethnic groups that were involved. People were wont to follow their own taste and styles of furnishing and decorating their homes that, in time, took on board Western and Dutch artworks and objects. The VOC was an active mediator for the transport of goods between various parts of Asia and were responsive to the differing demand for goods in the local situations they encountered.[19]

For our purpose, Michael North, in chapter "Domestic Interiors in Seventeenth- and Eighteenth-Century Batavia", looks into the Chinese

---

[18] The scholarship on the Dutch trading empire is vast. Recent works include Jan J. B. Kuipers, *De VOC: een multinational onder zeil, 1602–1799* (Zutphen: Walburg Pers, 2014); Lodewijk Wagenaar, *Aan de Overkant: ontmoetingen in dienst van de VOC en WIC 1600–1800* (Leiden: Sidestone Press, 2015); Robert Parthesius, *Dutch Ships in Tropical Waters: The Development of the Dutch East India Company (VOC) Shipping Network in Asia 1595–1660* (Amsterdam: Amsterdam University Press, 2007); M. A. P. Meilink-Roelofsz, M. E. van Opstall, and G. J. Schutte, eds., *Dutch Authors on Asian History* (Dordrecht: Foris Publications, 1988); Femme S. Gaastra, *The Dutch East India Company: Expansion and Decline* (Zutphen: Walburg Pers, 2003); and Kees Zandvliet, *The Dutch Encounter with Asia 1600–1950* (Zwolle: Rijksmuseum Amsterdam and Waanders Publishers, 2002).

[19] Thomas DaCosta Kaufmann and Michael North, eds., *Mediating Netherlandish Art and Material Culture in Asia* (Amsterdam: Amsterdam University Press, 2014), 12–13.

and Muslim homes in the cosmopolitan colonial city of Batavia. Intense market relations between Western Europe, Japan, China, and Southeast Asia resulted in periodic upticks of private art collecting from the late seventeenth and throughout the eighteenth century. Drawing on probate inventories, the registered lists of movable possessions left by deceased persons, North traces the patterns of household material acquisition, consumption, and taste. The Chinese primarily preferred to invest their wealth in labor, in slaves, and indentured laborers. Both Chinese and Muslims showed a marked inclination to spend lavishly on personal grooming and adornment. Expensive furnishings—beds, mirrors, and clocks—were the next priority. Only after these were acquired would paintings for the decoration of walls be considered.

North suggests that the broad emergence of a domestic material culture in Batavia followed distinct class and ethnic lines, though trends and preferences gradually conformed to a global material culture that came to be expressed in a similarity of tastes and fashions which could be observed across Europe, Asia, and North America. But what can be said of other consumption practices?

The sensory interest in traded goods was not limited to art, objects, or things that could not be physiologically enjoyed, as William G. Clarence-Smith's chapter "Betel, Tobacco and Beverages in Southeast Asia", the final essay in this collection, reminds us. Throughout Southeast Asia, chewing betel (*sirih*) was integral to religious ritual and social practices. It is an ancient and widespread practice, relished for its pleasurably intoxicating affects and pleasing aroma. Over time, however, this old and seemingly entrenched habit fell into steep decline. Since at least the mid-eighteenth century, European men in West Java who had adopted the habit, stopped chewing due largely to Dutch and British reformers' efforts to Westernize elite culture in Java. By the beginning of the twentieth century, as Western ideas of hygiene, civilization, and modernity spread, educated Indonesians and Filipinos had largely abandoned the habit.

As Clarence-Smith observes, the use and cultivation of tobacco introduced by the Iberians from the Americas in the late sixteenth century in the Philippines turned cigar smoking in the Philippines into something of a rage, while lower-class Indonesians preferred the local hand rolled fragrant cigarettes known as *kretek*. Other stimulants that successfully competed against the betel chew were hot beverages. Tea imported from China and India, transported and cultivated by Europeans, took hold and spread across mainland and maritime Southeast Asia, particularly among the expanding Chinese communities. Ethiopian Arabica coffee, grown in Yemen and western India was embraced in Java and beyond, with interventions by the VOC in the early seventeenth century; meanwhile, chocolate as a drink brought from the New World by Europeans to Dutch, Sri Lanka, and Spanish Philippines, diffused to parts of the Indonesian archipelago, by the mid-nineteenth century. The transformation in taste and the shift away from age-old consumption habits, as Clarence-Smith demonstrates, was the result of long processes of cultural mediation among several actors that included Europeans, mercantile agents, ethnic groups, and social classes. But also, significantly, as he argues, via the promotion of proselytizing religions, from Buddhists who favored tea-drinking, Muslim coffee drinkers, and Catholic clerics and, interestingly, local women, who enthusiastically took to drinking chocolate.

This book is concerned with the more quotidian diffusion of trade goods and objects and their impact on local communities, of the role played by the host of intermediaries who facilitated the processes, and of the small but significant changes wrought on aspects of everyday life and sensibilities. Europeans were major players in the transformation of material culture in Asia. They acted as mediators between different cultures and societies, transporting raw materials and finished objects from one place to another within Asia, and beyond. To a significant degree, it was often through the mediation of such items that they effected change and not just simply by introducing European cultural goods, or through their involvement as principal agents. Diffusion and the circulation of imported goods affected the cultural fabric of communities, led to local, sometimes dramatic and visually spectacular cultural innovation, as in the case of religious architecture, and to changes in categories of perception, aesthetics, and representations.

Japanese Export Lacquer and Global Art History: An Art of Mediation in Circulation

Thomas DaCosta Kaufmann

Abstract Japanese export lacquer was enmeshed in a complex network of commercial and artistic relations. Raw materials were brought from Southeast Asia to Japan, where finished lacquerware was made for export. Japanese export lacquer adapted Chinese and Indian decorative techniques, as well as European designs for motifs, forms, and functions. Chinese or Ryukyuan junks along with Spanish, Portuguese, and Dutch ships carried lacquer to places in Asia, Europe, and the Americas, where it was adopted and emulated. Lacquer thus provides a prime example of an art of mediation that involved Europeans and Asians in processes of circulation in the global history of art.

Keywords Japan · Lacquerware · Inter-Asian trade · Global trade · Art history

T. D. Kaufmann (✉)
Department of Art and Archaeology,
Princeton University, Princeton, NJ, USA

Introduction

How is the history of European-Asian cultural relations during the early modern era (roughly 1500–1800 CE) to be written? Approaches to the subject have altered radically in recent years, as scholars now regard interpretations stressing Western colonialism and imperialism as inappropriate for considerations of a time when Europeans were by no means dominant in Asian lands. A major reorientation in thinking about economic relations has also taken place, as André Gunder Frank's arguments highlight.[1] Frank challenged the older model of center and periphery that put Europe at the center and regarded the rest of the world as its periphery. He in effect reversed the model, arguing that Asian economies were central during the early modern period. This thesis is supported by the massive European export of bullion (much of it obtained from the Americas) to China and Japan (and India), for which luxuries (tea, silk, etc.) and finished artifacts were obtained. The familiar paradigm of economic imperialism (ultimately deriving from Karl Marx's *Das Kapital*) is thus turned on its head.[2] Two outstanding historians have even gone so far as to characterize the role of Europeans in Asia at this time as follows: 'Europeans crawled like lice on the hide of the continent' of Asia.[3] More broadly speaking, the place given to Asia in global history (and art history) has increased[4] while the impact of Europeans has been shown to be disparate in different parts of the world.[5]

However, to continue the metaphor, lice can spread disease. Europeans may have had an impact in Asia (and elsewhere), even if their

---

[1] André Gunder Frank, *Reorient. Global Economy in the Asian Age* (Berkeley: University of California Press, 1998).

[2] This is of course the way that contemporary Chinese in the period of the Ming dynasty might have liked to have seen their 'middle kingdom' (central country, *Zhongguo*): see Craig Clunas, *Empire of Great Brightness. Visual and Material Cultures of Ming China, 1368–1644* (London: Reaktion, 2007), 74.

[3] Leonard Blussé and Felipe Fernández Armesto, "Introduction," in *Shifting Communities and Identity Formation in Early Modern Asia*, ed. Leonard Blussé and Felipe Fernandez Armesto (Leiden: CNWA, 2003), 2.

[4] For relations between Asia and Latin America, see, for example, the essays collected in *Asia and Spanish America. Trans-Pacific Artistic and Cultural Exchange, 1500–1850*, ed. Donna Pierce and Ronal Otsuka (Denver: Denver Art Museum, 2009).

[5] See Serge Gruzinski, *L'aigle et le dragon: démesure européenne et mondialisation au XVIe siècle* (Paris: Fayard, 2012).

'influence' may be regarded negatively. This is admitted even in interpretations that seem to parallel those holding Europeans responsible for spreading devastating diseases to the Americas, or for the worldwide institutionalization of slavery involving Africans.[6] Without entering into debates about such questions, one may still ask what other roles Europeans played in global art history.

The present chapter suggests one answer. Results of research on the impact of the Dutch East India Company (or the VOC, its initials in Dutch) on material culture and art in Southern Africa and Asia have demonstrated that while Europeans may not have had an overwhelming impact on individual societies in Asia, they nevertheless played an important role in mediating cultures.[7] This analysis coincides with the replacement of center-periphery and other similar models of hierarchical relations with treatments of Europe and Asia as having 'connected' histories.[8] The dynamics connecting different cultures are rather to be seen as representing circulations in the global history of art.[9]

Mediation is here construed in relation to several processes of exchange. Europeans were involved in the transport of raw materials from one place to another in Asia, where these materials were used to manufacture luxury objects. The resultant products combined European

---

[6] Blussé and Fernández-Armesto, ibid., 3. This approach seems to follow some lines established by the well-known book by Alfred W. Crosby, *The Columbian Exchange. Biological and Cultural Consequences of 1492* (Westport, CT: Greenwood, 1972).

[7] See Thomas DaCosta Kaufmann and Michael North, "Introduction: Mediating Cultures," in *Mediating Netherlandish Art and Material Culture in Asia*, ed. Thomas DaCosta Kaufmann and Michael North (Amsterdam: Amsterdam University Press; Chicago and London: University of Chicago Press, 2014), 7–20, and also *eidem*, "Introduction—Artistic and Cultural Exchanges Between Europe and Asia, 1400–1900: Rethinking Markets, Workshops and Collections," in *Artistic and Cultural Exchanges Between Europe and Asia, 1400–1900. Rethinking Markets, Workshops and Collections*, ed. Michael North (Farnham and Burlington, VT: Ashgate, 2010), 1–8. For the notion of mediation as used here see further Astrid Erll, "Circulating Art and Material Culture: A Model of Transcultural Mediation," in *Mediating Netherlandish Art and Material Culture in Asia*, 321–28.

[8] See Jean-Louis Margolin and Claude Markovits, *Les Indes et L'Europe. Histoires connectées XVe–XXIe siècle* (Paris: Gallimard, 2015); Sanjay Subrahmanyam, *Explorations in Connected Histories* (New Delhi: Oxford University Press, 2005), 2 vols.

[9] See Thomas DaCosta Kaufmann, Catherine Dossin, and Béatrice Joyeux-Prunel, *Circulations in the Global History of Art* (Aldershot and Burlington, VT: Ashgate, 2015).

and Asian sources that affected the types, forms, functions, and meanings of objects; they have accordingly been described as mixtures.[10] European and Asian intermediaries carried these artifacts from one part of Asia to another, and also to Europe, where they were distributed farther. Techniques of manufacture along with the materials and the products transported circulated in a larger network: Europeans brought goods to Africa (especially cloths), and to the Americas. Asian-made objects thus conveyed motifs, designs, or functions, to different contexts, where they were further adopted, adapted, and emulated. This process constitutes a global pattern of circulation, wherein silver (ultimately from Upper Peru or Mexico) was traded for objects of Asian provenance but often having European involvement or interventions that then went elsewhere in Asia, Europe, and the Americas.

Lacquerware represents one such art of mediation. The present chapter reexamines scientific analyses of lacquer, documents pertaining to the lacquer trade, and individual objects. It considers lacquer made in Japan as exemplifying circulations in the global history of art.

THE PLACE OF LACQUER

Traces of materials related to lacquer have been found in China in objects that are over 6000 years old. Highly crafted artifacts using lacquer are evinced from at least the time of the Shang dynasty (ca. 1600–1100 BCE). Following its early use in China, artisans in several other parts of East Asia (Japan, Korea, Ryukyu Islands) also utilized lacquer in the manufacture of luxury items.[11] Long before the arrival of Europeans lacquer objects also circulated in East and Southeast Asia.[12] The advent

---

[10] Notably as 'hybrid' or 'mestizo': for an overview of the first of these notions see Peter Burke, *Cultural Hybridity* (Cambridge, MA: Polity, 2009). For 'mestizo' cultures see most notably the work of Serge Gruzinski, expanded to the global dimension in *Les Quatre Parties du Monde. Histoire d'une mondialisation* (Paris: La Marinière, 2004).

[11] There is an extensive bibliography on lacquer: a good introduction to the varieties and antiquity of Asian lacquer is provided by James C. Y. Watt and Barbara B. Ford, *East Asian Lacquer, the Florence and Herbert Irving Collection* (New York: Metropolitan Museum of Art, 1991).

[12] See Kaori Hidaka, "Maritime Trade in Asia and the Circulation of Lacquerware," in *East Asian Lacquer: Material Culture, Science and Conservation* (London: Victoria and Albert Museum, 2011), 6–8.

of the Spanish and Portuguese in the early sixteenth century turned lacquerware into a trade good that was even more widely diffused throughout Asia, Europe, and the Americas.[13]

The arrival of Europeans in East Asia also affected the development of new shapes, decorative patterns, iconography, and techniques in the production of lacquerware. Probably from the second decade of the sixteenth century, new sorts of fine wares of various kinds were made for export to Europe.[14] The Japanese produced lacquerware for the Spanish and Portuguese, *nanban* or *namban* as the Japanese called them, meaning southern Barbarians, since Iberians first arrived via the Ryukyu Islands. Japanese lacquerware made for the Portuguese and Spanish is consequently known as *nanban shikki*.[15]

Numerous pieces of *nanban urushi*, to use another Japanese word, *urushi*, for lacquer, were made for the Jesuits, and also by them in workshops they directed in Japan.[16] Many such objects incorporate pearl, *raden*, inlaid or sprinkled with gold and silver on the black lacquer background, a process known as *maki-e*, as was already employed in Japanese

[13] For an introduction to the networks established, see Etsuko Miyata Rodriguez, "The Early Manila Galleon Trade: Merchants' Networks and Markets in Sixteenth- and Seventeenth-Century Mexico," in *Asia and Spanish America*, 37–57.

[14] The fullest account of Japanese export ware is O. P. Impey and C. J. A. Jörg, *Japanese Export Lacquer 1580–1850* (Amsterdam: Hotei, 2005), incorporating and superseding earlier studies by Impey, and with full bibliography to the date of publication. See further for early lacquer made for Europe, Annemarie Jordan Gschwend, "O Fascínio de Cipango. Artes Decorativas e lacas da Ásia Oriental em Portugal, Espanha e Áustria (1511–1598)," in *Os Construtores do Oriente Português* (Porto: Edifico da Alfâmdega, 1998), 195–223.

[15] For the general question of *nanban* art and the reciprocal influences of Iberians on Japanese art and Japanese art in Iberia see *Arte Namban. Influencia española y portuguesa en el arte japonés siglos xvi y xvii* (Madrid: Museo del Prado, 1981); Maria Helena Mendes Pinto, *Biombos Namban/Namban Screens* (Lisbon: Museu Nacional de Arte Antiga, 1986); *Traje Namban* (Lisbond: Muso de Arte Antiga, 1994); and *Biombos Namban/Namban Screens* (Porto: Museu Nacional de Soares dos Reis, 2009). For lacquerware, see especially *Lacas Namban: huellas de Japón en España: IV Centenario de la Embajada Keichō = Namban Lacquer: Japan Remained in Spain: 400 Years After the Keicho Embassy* (Madrid: Ministerio de Educación, Cultura y Deporte, Fundación Japón, 2013).

[16] The fullest recent account of Jesuit workshops in Japan, using sources from Japanese as well as Western European languages, though focusing on paintings, is Noriko Kotani, "Studies in Jesuit art in Japan" (PhD dissertation, Princeton University, 2010), now being prepared for publication.

lacquer.[17] Lacquer identifiable as being made for export however also often employs a new foliate decorative pattern. Several other characteristics identify *nanban* ware. These include shapes and purposes (coffers, lecterns, altars) not previously known in Japan, as well as European coats of arms or religious symbols, including the monogram of the name of Jesus to whom the Society of Jesus was dedicated. Some of these objects specifically served Christian religious purposes, notably the production of lecterns and pyxes, boxes for the reserved Eucharistic host[18] (Fig. 1). So-called viatic pyxes were used to transport the host to the sick; in the Americas they were also employed to transport the host to *visitas* (chapels used for services but lacking regular priests), or for other ritual devotional purposes.

The Jesuits encouraged production of *nanban* wares for religious functions, which they could have served in Japan until their expulsion, and also for export to other parts of the world. Even such a well-known story as that of the martyrs of Nagasaki, in which Franciscans and Jesuit missionaries were put to death in 1597, attests to their international origins (the martyrs included people from Mexico, Europe, India, and Japan) and their early involvement in trade as well as in politics. (The Franciscans and Jesuits were punished not just because of their beliefs, and their entanglement in local politics, but because they were caught embroiled in what local authorities regarded as illicit trade, commerce connected independently without the permission of local authorities.)[19] After the Jesuits and other Catholic orders were expelled from Japan, the Dutch East India Company (VOC) assumed the role of intermediaries in the lacquer trade.[20]

---

[17] For a general discussion of the use of mother-of-pearl in lacquer, see Denise Patry Leidy, *Mother-of-Pearl. A Tradition in Asian Lacquer* (New York: Metropolitan Museum of Art, 2006).

[18] For two such objects see Nuno Vassallo e Silva, "A Companhia de Jesus e as artes decorativas no Oriente português," in *Arte Oriental nas Colecções do Museu de São Roque* (Lisbon: Santa Casa da Misericórdia, 2010), 21, Figs. 5 and 6. For a definition of pyxes and their uses, see Thomas DaCosta Kaufmann "Pyxes and Ciboria," in *Eucharistic Vessels of the Middle Ages* (Cambridge, MA: Busch-Reisinger Museum, 1975; New York: Garland, 1977 [2nd ed.]), 65–68.

[19] See John Nelson, "Myths, Missions, and Mistrust. The Fate of Christianity in Sixteenth and Seventeenth Century Japan," *History and Anthropology* 13, no. 2 (2002): 93–111.

[20] For a good brief account of the Dutch involvement in the lacquer trade, see Christiaan J. A. Jörg, "Dutch VOC Records as a Source for dating 17th Century Japanese Export

Fig. 1 Pyx for Communion Hosts, Japan, Momoyama Period, late sixteenth century, black lacquered cryptomeria wood decorated with gold and silver power and inlaid with mother-of-pearl, Lisbon, Museo de Arte Antiga, inv. 18 cx © Lisbon, Museo de Arte Antiga, Direção-Geral do Património Cultural/Arquivo de Documentação Fotográfica (DGPC/ADF)

During the early modern period, lacquerware produced in Japan was coveted in many places in the world. In addition to its religious uses, collectors in Europe and in the Americas collected it and employed it

Lacquer," in *After the Barbarians. Namban Works of Art for the Japanese, Portuguese and Dutch Markets* (London and Lisbon: Jorge Welsh, 2007), 42–50; see also in general Impey and Jörg, *Japanese Export Lacquer*.

in various ways, as discussed below. Emperors of the Qing Dynasty in China, and perhaps earlier emperors, were among its ardent collectors.[21] Present-day collectors of Asian art still cherish lacquer objects made in Japan.[22]

Furthermore, in addition to the metamorphosis of forms, imagery, and functions, the raw materials involved in the production of lacquer, especially 'Japanese export lacquer,' their transportation, and their use in the manufacture, trade, consumption, and collecting of works made in Japan relate to several connected histories. While the story of other luxury materials might be treated similarly, lacquer allows for many insights into complex patterns of circulations of commerce, materials, and artifacts that encompass Southeast Asia, South Asia, East Asia, Europe, and the Americas. In any instance, although it was not produced in the huge quantities of porcelain,[23] the amount of lacquer manufactured for export as well as its quality is noteworthy.

The study of lacquer in general and of Japanese lacquer has engaged the attention of many scholars.[24] But much more remains to be said.[25] Most important, the interpretation of objects and their technical examination allow for a fuller reconsideration of the ways in which lacquer participated in the art of mediation, the term art being used to describe the circulation of items as well as the actual objects exchanged. To begin at the beginning, the actual materials used to make lacquer in Japan reveal that more went into the production of 'Japanese' export lacquer than may at first meet the eye.

---

[21] Huixia Chen, *Qing gong shi hui: yuan cang Riben qi qi te zhan/Japanese Lacquer from the Ch'ing Court Collection* (Taipei: Chu ban, 2002).

[22] As exemplified by the trade in such goods carried on by Jorge Welsh (see note 20).

[23] For Japanese (and Chinese) porcelain and its circulation, see most recently Robert Finlay, *The Pilgrim Art. Cultures of Porcelain in World History* (Berkeley, Los Angeles, and London: University of California Press, 2010), and *Chinese and Japanese Porcelain for the Dutch Golden Age*, ed. Jan van Campen and Titus Eliëns (Zwolle: Waanders, 2014).

[24] See the bibliography in Impey and C. J. A. Jörg, *Japanese Export Lacquer.*

[25] Cynthia Viallé, "Japanese Lacquer Cabinets in the Records of the Dutch East India Company," in *Japanische Lackkunst für Bayerns Fürsten. Die Japanischen Lackmöbel der Staatlichen Münzsammlung*, ed. Anton Schweizer et al. (Munich: Staatlichen Münzsammlung, 2011), 31–46; *eadem*, "Fit for Kings and Princes: A Gift of Japanese Lacquer," in *Large and Broad. The Dutch Impact on Early Modern Asia. Essays in Honor of Leonard Blussé*, ed. Nagazumi Yōko (Tokyo: The Toyo Bunko, 2010), 188–222; *eadem*,

MATERIALS AND FORMS IN MOTION

Other lands also played roles in the production and circulation of materials used for lacquerware as well as the designs found on it. Mother-of-pearl inlay was traditionally employed to make luxury goods in India, and it is possible that the material itself, or some of it, was brought thence as part of trade with Japan. It is also possible that some of the silver and gold used for dust and inlay in lacquer manufacture derived from the Americas, whence much of these precious metals originated that were brought to East Asia. While this hypothesis remains speculative, Southeast Asia was and is an important source for the basic raw material used in Japanese lacquerware, namely for the actual plant material used to make lacquered objects.[26] Lacquer sap from Southeast Asia was utilized not just for local production in that region, but also supplied the basic constituent for the manufacture of much lacquerware in Japan. Southeast Asia was moreover home to several major harbors such as Manila, Batavia (now Jakarta), and Malacca, through which goods also passed (e.g., from India or Europe, and ultimately from the Americas) on their way to and from Japan. Furthermore, Southeast Asia was itself a receiver of lacquerware as a well as a producer—although, as will be argued here, it also remains more speculative if objects made in the area of Myanmar (Burma), Cambodia, or Thailand, rather than in Japan, as distinct from the raw material itself, were exchanged within Asia and exported to Europe and to the Americas. And techniques, forms of manufacture,[27] as well as motifs conveyed by other Asians and Europeans circulated in Japan.[28]

"Two Boxes and Two Balustrades; Private Orders for Fine Japanese Export Lacquer," in *East Asian Lacquer: Material Culture, Science and Conservation*, ed. Shayne Rivers, Rupert Faulkner, and Boris Pretzel (London: Victoria and Albert Museum and Archetype, 2011).

[26] For a good general introduction see Miho Kitagawa, "Materials, Tools and Techniques Used on Namban Lacquerwork," in *After the Barbarians*, 70–88. See also Femke Diercks, "Inspired by Asia. Responses in the Dutch Decorative Arts," in *Aisa in Amsterdam. The Culture of Luxury in the Golden Age*, ed. Karina H. Corrigan et al. (Salem, MA: Peabody Essex Museum; Amsterdam: Rijksmuseum; New Haven and London: Yale University Press, 2015), especially 246–47.

[27] See Pedro Cancela de Abreu, "The Construction Techniques of Namban Objects," in *After the Barbarians*, 52–68.

[28] As discussed in general by Pedro Moura Carvalho, "The Circulation of European and Asian Works of Art in Japan, circa 1600," in *Portugal, Jesuits and Japan. Spiritual Beliefs and Earthly Goods*, ed. Victoria Weston (Boston: McMullen Museum of Art, Boston College, 2013), 37–43.

The basic material that provides the source for lacquer derives from the sap of three types of tree found in Asia. In Japan, as in China and Korea, sap may be taken directly from a variety of the *rhus vernicifera*, also known as the *rhus verniciflua*. The particular species that supplies the sap used for lacquer is the *toxicodendron vernicifluum*. As the Latin nomenclature (vernicifera = varnish bearing; vernciflua = varnish flowing) implies, sap from the tree is used to make a viscous fluid that is called *urushi* in Japan, and *qi* in China. The sap is scraped from the tree, homogenized, and hydrogen is extracted from it. The resulting substance then hardens on contact with the air. Having hardened, it is used to cover objects. This sort of lacquer has long been utilized to produce fine objects in China, Japan, and Korea. As suggested, the use of lacquer in Japan may be further distinguished by the fixation of gold and other metallic powders, a process known as *maki-e*; *maki-e* often has mother-of-pearl inlay.[29] This technique with mother-of-pearl and metallic power is seen on many sixteenth- seventeenth-, and eighteenth-century objects, including those with traditional decorative patterns, among them chrysanthemums, Japanese *kiku*. Such patterns relate perhaps to a Japanese emblem (*mon*) that often is associated with the imperial house; they may indicate that objects so adorned were originally made for domestic consumption (although they also may also have been sold abroad, as a sign of their provenance). Other aspects of *maki-e* technique including both the use of silver dust and of mother-of-pearl inlay were initially derived from Chinese and Korean prototypes,[30] while the types of motifs, forms, and functions of objects, were also influenced by Europeans.

The species of lacquer trees indigenous to East Asia itself (China, Korea, Japan) is however not the only one used as a supply for lacquer. Sap that has been tapped from trees that grow in Southeast Asia is also utilized for lacquer. In Myanmar and Thailand trees of the species *gluta*

---

[29] The process is frequently described: a good recent account with illustrations is offered in Meiko Nagashima, "Japanese Lacquers Exported to Spanish America and Spain," in *Asia and Spanish America*, 107–17.

[30] See *Encompassing the Globe. Portugal and the World in the 16th and 17th Centuries. Reference Catalogue*, ed. Jay A. Levenson (Washington, DC: Smithsonian Institution, 2007), 164 (cat. J-6).

usitata (or *melanorrhoea usitata*) produce lacquer, and in Cambodia (and Vietnam) those of the species *gluta lacifera* tree (also known as *rhus succedanea*). These kinds of Southeast Asian lacquers are known as *thitsi* lacquer, from a local name for the tree; Europeans, especially the Dutch, called them black lacquer (a name that corresponds to the older Greek generic appellation, *melanorrhoea*, meaning black-flowing) or *namrack*. In Myanmar, lacquer was used for an extensive and long-lasting production of what is known in Europe as Burmese lacquerware.[31] Although probably originating at a later date than those made elsewhere in Asia, lacquer objects were also produced in Thailand, whence some also entered Western European collections.[32]

It has been demonstrated that so-called *thitsi* lacquer was also employed in the production of Japanese lacquerware, specifically for the making of Japanese export lacquer. Chromatographic analysis of a lacquer vase from the sixteenth or seventeenth century considered a Valuable Cultural Property that was found in ruins in Kyoto has determined that it contained *melanorrhoea* (or *gluta*) *usitata*. This discovery provides clear evidence for the use of raw materials from Southeast Asia in the manufacture of lacquer in Japan.[33]

Furthermore, scientific analysis of four eighteenth-century pieces of French furniture (Getty Museum, Los Angeles) in which Japanese export lacquer has been inserted has indicated Southeast Asian lacquer was also

---

[31] See Ralph Isaacs and T. Richard Blurton, *Visions from the Golden Land: Burma and the Art of Lacquer* (London: British Museum, 2000); Uta Weigelt, *Birmas Lackkunst in deutschen Museen* (Münster: Museum für Lackkunst, 2005); and Ralph Isaacs, Sylvia Fantin-lu, Catherine Reymond, and Than Thon U, *Lacque et or de Birmanie* (Milan: Silvana, 2011).

[32] See, for example, Gunter Rudolf Diesinger, *Ostasiatische Lackarbeiten sowie Arbeiten aus Europa, Thailand und Indien* (Braunschweig: Herzog Anton Ulrich-Museum, 1990), 257–63.

[33] Takayuji Honda, Rong Lu, Nobuhiko Kitanto, Yoshimi Kamiya, and Tetsuo Miyakoshi, "Applied Analysis and Identification of Ancient Lacquer Based on Pyrolysis-Gas Chromatography/Mass," *Journal of Applied Polymer Science* 118 (2010): 897–901. See further the essays in *Japanische und europäische Lackarbeiten: Rezeption, Adaption, Restaurierung: Deutsch-Japanisches Forschungsprojekt zur Untersuchung und Restaurierung historischer Lacke, gefördert durch das Bundesministerium für Bildung, Wissenschaft, Forschung und Technologie = Japanese and European Lacquerware: Adoption, Adaptation, Conservation*, ed. Michael Kühlenthal (Munich: Bayerisches Landesamt für Denkmalpflege, 2000).

used for products made in Japan but sent abroad. Chemical components related to *gluta usitata* have been found in layers of samples where they show it has been mixed with *urushi*. Significantly, samples taken from all four of the pieces examined reveal chemicals identifiable with so-called *thitsi* lacquer that has been mixed with *urushi* lacquer. The works studied were all composed of Japanese lacquer that must have been made during the second half of the seventeenth century. Because of the French composition of the furniture in the eighteenth century, and the fact that Japan had been closed to all Europeans but the Dutch since ca. 1640, and the continuing conflicts between the French and the Spanish, the individual pieces of lacquer themselves were most likely transported to Europe by the Dutch; hence they may be regarded as resulting from the export trade in luxuries in which the Dutch served as intermediaries. This discovery suggests not only that Southeast Asian lacquer may have been combined with East Asian lacquer to make objects. The fact that all the pieces analyzed reveal this combination leads to the inference that this process of manufacture may have been used extensively in the production of Japanese export lacquer.

In addition, wood oil has been found in three of the pieces sampled in the Getty project. This is resin derived from trees of the genus *Dipterocarpus*, which also grow in Southeast Asia. This oil would probably have been used to thin the *thitsi* lacquer, and the *urushi* lacquer as well, if it were too thick.

Various reasons may be proposed for the use of Southeast Asian lacquer, and consequently of wood oil from the region. Evidently local supplies of the raw material in Japan were not sufficient to meet demands for production. The amount of sap that can be extracted from individual *rhus vernicifera* trees is limited. Prices demanded by the local Japanese suppliers, and accordingly manufacturers were thus high. The Dutch (and the Portuguese before them) were pressed on the one hand to maintain or establish a viable profit margin; on the other hand they were compelled to keep prices of the finished goods relatively low at home because of economies of scale.[34] Yet they had to maintain a standard of quality, to make lacquerware attractive for purchase, and to keep it competitive especially in the later seventeenth and eighteenth century when

---

[34] See Impey and Jörg, *Japanese Export Lacquer*, 95.

many European imitations were made, a large topic.[35] One may speculate that a similar problem may have affected Spanish trade with the Americas, where imitations were also produced (Fig. 3). Frequent haggling resulted in extensive negotiations in Japan. In such conditions, the use of more copious and less expensive materials would have been attractive.[36]

But how did the Southeast Asian components arrive in Japan? On one end, records of the trading station of the Dutch East India Company (the VOC) in Myanmar indicate that substantial amounts of *thitsi* lacquer, because the Burmese variety was considered the highest quality, were shipped to Japan. They averaged 4000 pounds annually between 1650 and 1680, with as much as 12,000 pounds being sent in a single year. Sales of *namrack*, the Dutch name for this lacquer, brought the VOC large profits in Japan.[37] Similarly, shipments were made of wood oil from Burma to Japan that average 500 jugs annually for the period 1660–1680.[38] These would also have been employed to make laquer. On the receiving end in Japan, *Dagregisters*, the daily records, of shipping to Deshima, the Dutch island factory (trading post) in Nagasaki harbor, indicate that as early as 1635 *thitsi* lacquer was arriving from Burma and being sold to makers of export lacquerware.[39] Records for the years from 1636 to 1643 indicate that large amounts of lacquer, called black lacquer, were being shipped by the Dutch East India Company from Cambodia and Siam.[40] Although after 1641 the shipments could have passed via Malacca after the Dutch seized it, they would no doubt have also been

---

[35] For examples of these from an early European collection see Diesinger, *Ostasiatische Lackarbeiten*.

[36] See in general for the information in these paragraphs Arlen Heginbotham and Michael Schilling, "New Evidence for the use of Southeast Asian Raw materials in Seventeenth-century Japanese Export Lacquer," in *East Asian Lacquer: Material Culture, Science and Conservation*.

[37] Wil. O. Dijk, *Seventeenth-Century Burma and the Dutch East India Company* (Singapore: NIAS Press, 2006), 125–26; Appendix V (cd), 82.

[38] Heginbotham and Schilling, "New Evidence"; however, Dijk, *Burma*, Appendix 5, 92, reports that most wood oil exported by the Dutch went to Batavia (Jakarta) where it was probably used for ships.

[39] Heginbotham and Schilling, "New Evidence," 8.

[40] As recorded abundantly in *Dagregisters/Diaries Kept by the Heads of the Dutch Factory in Japan* (Tokyo: Daigaku Siryo Hensanjo: 1974–2007), 11 vols., *passim*.

shipped via Batavia/Jakarta, the hub of Dutch trade, in any case. Along the way they may have passed by Taiwan (held by the Dutch between the 1620s and early 1660s) as well; Taiwanese goods are often mentioned in conjunction with the shipments of lacquer in the documents from Deshima, and there is evidence for such cross-shipment of lacquerware from Japan.[41]

Similar conditions to those affecting Dutch trade applied to the earlier manufacture of *nanban* lacquerware that circulated in the Lusophone world.[42] A remarkable Japanese lacquerware object (Private Collection) regarded as a *nanban* commission reveals a similar constitution to the Getty furniture. This is a bed with typical *nanban urushi* patterns employing *maki-e* with inlaid mother-of-pearl. Its headboard moreover contains spaces reserved for emblematic decorative elements that resemble the *mon* heraldic patterns found in Japan. These characteristics strongly suggest that is an example of *nanban shikki*, a lacquer work made in Japan for export, since beds were not traditionally used in Japan. The headboard of the bed also is decorated with an arcaded pattern known from Iberian furniture of the sixteenth and seventeenth centuries, allowing for approximate dating.

Technical examination of the bed indicates that it again employs lacquer from Southeast Asia.[43] This detail also suggests another reason for the import of Southeast Asian lacquer: it was in demand for goods produced for export by the Portuguese as well as by the Dutch. Since the dating indicates a period before Dutch involvement with Japanese export lacquer, the existence of this bed points to the connection of the Portuguese in an unexpected light, revealing another level of complexity in the lacquer trade.

---

[41] *De Dagregisters van het Kasteel Zeelandia, Taiwan, 1629–1662*, ed. J. L. Blussé, M. E. van Opstall, and Ts'ao Yung-ho, with the collaboration of Chiang Shu-sheng and W. Milde (The Hague: M. Nijhoff, 1986–2000) *passim*. See below for an example of Japanese lacquer shipped via Taiwan.

[42] It should be recalled that while places like Goa, Malacca, and Macao were in Portuguese hands, from 1580–1640 the king of Spain was also king of Portugal.

[43] See the entry by Alexandra Curvelo in *Encomendas Namban. Os Portugueses no Japão da Idade Moderna/Namban Commissions. The Portuguese in Modern Age Japan* (Lisbon: Museu Fundação Oriente, 2010), 160 (cat. no. 40); unfortunately, the entry does not indicate if traces of Japanese lacquer were found mixed with that of Southeast Asian lacquer. See also *eadem*, "Nanban Art: What's Past in Prologue," in *Portugal, Jesuits and Japan*, 76.

INTRA-ASIAN TRADE AND LACQUERWARE

Beds are known to have been brought by the Portuguese to Japan, where they may have served as a source for imitation suggested by this object.[44] But the bed in question has a provenance traceable to Goa, the capital of the Portuguese viceroyalty and their main enclave in India.[45] It thus had probably been sent from Japan to India; the transport of beds made in East Asia to India is documented.[46] *Leitos*, beds, were especially important as luxurious forms of decoration in Goa.[47] They would have been so regarded also because beds were relatively unknown in India. A *nanban* bed in a European style might have seemed especially impressive.

The existence of this bed offers direct evidence for the involvement of the Portuguese and Spanish in the intra-Asian trade in lacquerware, specifically in the transportation of objects from Japan to India.[48] Many documents suggest that lacquerware from Japan was carried by the Portuguese both to their own enclaves, and probably to the Mughal court as well. In addition, there is also documentary evidence that the Dutch conveyed *nanban* lacquerware to India before the Portuguese were expelled from Japan.[49]

---

[44] Curvelo, *Encomendas*, 155–60.

[45] Curvelo, ibid., 158.

[46] Curvelo, ibid., 156, cites a document from 1563.

[47] I owe this information to a communication from Maria Cristina Osswald, who has made an intensive study of the archives in Goa. Osswald's most comprehensive work on Jesuit architecture in Goa and their features has been published as Cristina Osswald, *Written in Stone. Jesuit Buildings in Goa and Their Artistic and Architectural Features* (Goa: Goa 1556 and Golden Heart Emporium Bookshop, 2013). See further for the Goan milieu Paulo Varela Gomes, *Whitewash, Redstone. A History of Church Architecture in Goa* (New Delhi: Yoda Press, 2011).

[48] For the creation of lacquer objects for the Portuguese and Dutch markets as well as for local Japanese one, see Teresa Canepa, "Namban Works of Art for the Japanese, Portuguese and Dutch Markets," in *After the Barbarians*, 14–29, and Alexandra Curvelo, "The Black Ship," ibid., 30–40.

[49] See Jordan Gschwend, "O Fascínio"; Impey and Jörg, *Japanese Export Lacquer*, 235–36 for the Spanish. See also Impey and Jörg, ibid., 232–35, for the Portuguese. Early Dutch trade in *nanban* lacquer, perhaps initiated by the Portuguese, is considered, ibid., 242–45.

Lacquerware was probably already known in India through earlier Chinese and perhaps through Southeast Asian artifacts, but not in the refined form evinced by Japanese *nanban* lacquerware. Japanese objects could moreover only have become largely familiar in South Asia through the European opening of trade routes to Japan, because of the previous absence of direct routes, and because Southeast Asian and Chinese goods carried on their vessels would probably have excluded them in any case. The Portuguese involvement in transporting *nanban* wares to India as well as the early and later Dutch involvement in the Indian trade may be considered in this context. Documents indicate that during the mid- and later seventeenth century, after direct Portuguese contact with Japan had been broken, the Dutch East India Company brought many pieces of Japanese lacquer to various parts of India, including gifts intended for the court of the Great Mughal and other potentates.[50]

In this light, one may also reconsider two well-known Mughal miniatures that depict Europeans carrying lacquerware. Both are found in the Windsor *Padshanama*, an imperial Mughal manuscript documenting the reign of Shah Jahan (ruled 1628–1658). One image (fol. 117a; Fig. 2), painted ca. 1634, depicts the capture of Port Hoogly (Hugly), a Portuguese factory relatively near modern Kolkata (Calcutta) that took place June–October 1632. It shows the Portuguese fleeing from their fort. A detail at the top right of the miniature shows some Europeans and an Asian handling a box whose black and gold decoration is characteristic of lacquer patterns. This box is obviously being handled as a precious item, because it is uniquely shown as being worth saving. Another miniature (fol. 116b) depicts an event of July 1633, although it may have been painted ca. 1650. It shows a group of Europeans at the court of Shah Jahan in Agra, where they are waiting in attendance outside his Jharoka (audience chamber) in the Diwan-i-Am (audience hall) of the Red Fort there. One of the Europeans also holds a box in his hands. This box is also depicted as being black and gold, hence identifiable as a typical lacquer-ware product. Since the other Europeans are carrying jewels on pillows, the box must be regarded similarly as a precious object worthy of being presented at the Mughal court. The

---

[50] Impey and Jörg, *Japanese Export Lacquer*, 251–64.

Fig. 2 Portuguese escaping from a mined building at Hoogly, detail of *The Capture of Port Hoogly*, c. 1634, Padshanameh, Royal Library, Windsor Castle, fol. 117r, RCIN 1005025 Royal Collection Trust/© Her Majesty Queen Elizabeth II 2018

Europeans may have been ambassadors, although they have also been interpreted as Portuguese prisoners from Hugly. Whatever their ultimate identities, the significance of the presentation of lacquer objects remains the same: they were regarded as precious gifts for the Great Mughal.[51]

While several important scholars have identified the boxes as coming from East Asia and specifically as *nanban* ware,[52] it has also been suggested that they may be Bengali.[53] But the latter suggestion is

---

[51] For illustrations and identification of these images, see Milo Cleveland Beach and Ebba Koch, *King of the World. The Padshanama. An Imperial Mughal Manuscript from the Royal Library, Windsor Castle* (London: Azimuth, 1997; Washington, DC: Smithsonian Institution), 56–59 and 179–80.

[52] Jordan Gschwend, "O Fascínio de Cipango," 195; Koch, *King of the World*, 179.

[53] Pedro de Moura Carvalho, "Oriental Export Lacquerwares and Their Problematic Origin," in *Exotica. Portugals Entdeckungen im Spiegel fürstlicher Kunst- und Wunderkammer der Renaissance (Jahrbuch des kunsthistorischen Museums Wien* 3 (2000), ed. Helmut Trnek and Sabine Haag, 246–61; commentary on plate on 255. See further

implausible, because it is very doubtful that the Mughals would have regarded something as a valuable gift, and their artists would have recorded it as such, that Europeans had merely brought from nearby Bengal, rather than from farther away. The *Padshanama* miniature of Hugly also suggests that supposedly 'Bengali' lacquer was carried by the Portuguese away from Bengal, but why if it were really Bengali, rather than from another place, would it have been singled out as something special that the Portuguese would have thought worthy of being preserved? In any event, the facts that the lacquer objects were regarded as fitting gifts for an important ruler from whom one hoped to gain favor, and that similarly the box taken from Hugly was deemed worth rescuing, attest to the rarity and importance of these objects in European eyes, as seen through the acute observation of a Mughal artist, which a local Indian, Bengali, provenance would not have had. It is much more likely that the lacquer objects depicted in the *Padshanama* had a more 'exotic' provenance, from far-off Japan, and were not of Indian manufacture. (Nor for that matter do they resemble lacquer known from Burma/Myanmar.)

The suggestion that the boxes depicted were of Bengali origin derives from the hypothesis that an industry for lacquer production existed in India, in Bengal and on the Coromandel Coast. However, another good counter-argument is provided by objects actually known as 'Coromandel lacquer' or Coromandel screens in Europe. These are pieces of carved and painted lacquer, largely of Chinese manufacture, dating originally from the Ming dynasty (seventeenth century) that are so named because they were transported on ships to Europe that had as their place of embarkation the Coromandel or southeast coast of India. They were not of Indian manufacture; the provenance of lacquer objects from the Coromandel Coast was from East Asia.

Moreover, documents indicated that lacquer made by the Japanese was in fact transported to clients in Bengal. Objects are recorded as having been commissioned by the Dutch East India Company from lacquer makers in Japan to be used as boxes to contain betel, chewed in

---

Pedro Moura Carvalho, *Luxury for Export. Artistic Exchange Between India and Portugal Around 1600* (Boston: Isabella Stewart Gardner Museum, 2008), 30–33 (cat. no. 3).

South Asia and Southeast Asia. One such item was described in a letter of 1682 sent from a Dutchman in Bengal to Deshima.[54] This raises the possibility that lacquer associated with Bengal may have been made in Japan.

It seems that the only apparently sure basis for the hypothesis of the Indian origins for some lacquerware lies in the existence of pieces of lacquer made using Indian wood. But this argument is also insecure, because Indian wood in lacquerware, like that of wood from Korea that has also been found in Japanese lacquer boxes, could also have been carried to Japan.

It is known that the Mughals appreciated East Asian products, along with other items from all parts of the world that the Portuguese and later the Dutch) purveyed to them.[55] One familiar example is the long-standing taste in India for porcelain.[56] It is therefore likely that Europeans were responsible for introducing Japanese lacquerware to India, and that the *Padshanama* miniatures illustrate this process.[57]

One further note: the intra-Asian cycle of materials in which lacquerware circulated may be completed by recognition that Japanese export lacquer also went to Southeast Asia. They were carried there not only by

---

[54] "Langwerpige [beteldosen] in forme van een meloen," in a letter from Nicolaas Baukes to Hendrik Canzius in Deshima, Nationaal Archief, The Hague, archive of the Dutch factory in Japan, 1.04.21, inv. 313, Bengal; cited in an entry by Cynthia Viallé, *Asia in Amsterdam*, 114, n. 4.

[55] For the general impact of the Portuguese at the Mughal court, see *Goa and the Great Mughal*, ed. Jorge Flores and Nuno Vassallo e Silva (Lisbon: Calouste Gulbenkian Foundation; London: Scala, 2004). For the importation of objects by the Dutch to other courts in India see Sanjay Subrahmanyam, "Europeans in the Deccan," in *Sultans of Deccan India. Opulence and Fantasy*, ed. Navina Najat Haidar and Marika Sardar (New York: Metropolitan Museum of Art; New Haven and London Yale University Press, 2015), 309–12 and also 319–24 (cat. no. 193–96).

[56] See for an overview of this subject the many references in Robert Finlay, *The Pilgrim Art. Cultures of Porcelain in World History* (Berkeley, Los Angles, and London: University of California Press, 2010), 233–38, 245–48.

[57] Cf. Moura de Carvalho, *Luxury for Export*, 30–31. There is also another way to interpret the evidence for Indian production of lacquerware. Even assuming that it existed, for which as suggested we have no sure evidence, the Indian Bengali and Coromandel lacquer industry would have produced black and gold pieces, and imitated East Asian works, which would have been inspired by Japanese lacquerware. It should also be noted that there is no evidence for the export of Southeast Asian lacquer from Burma to India that has been found in the Dutch East India archives: see Dijk, *Seventeenth-century Burma*.

the Portuguese, but by the Dutch, who had established a factory of the East India Company in Ayutthaya, Thailand, in 1608.[58] The Dutch East India Company regularly sent orders from the Siamese court there to Deshima for Japanese lacquerware, whence it was shipped either directly back, or via Taiwan. A striking instance of this is an order made by the king in 1650 for betel boxes (such boxes and sets were regarded as signs of rank, and gifts of them were signs of royal favor) in the shape of melons.[59]

However, Japanese lacquerware did not always stay in Siam/Thailand. In one of the most striking cross-cultural encounters of the seventeenth century, a Siamese embassy of 1680 carried gifts not just of Siamese lacquerware, but large amounts of Japanese export lacquer to France. Indeed, this lacquer is described as being as variable quality.[60] This corresponds to what has been observed as a decline in the quality of Japanese export lacquer made after ca. 1640, which probably involved increased use of non-Japanese lacquer as the basis for its production.[61] Can this also mean, ironically, that the Siamese were receiving, and then passing on as gifts lacquer objects that had been made in Japan but that had used substantial amounts of raw lacquer from Siam or elsewhere in Southeast Asia?

Lacquer in the Wider World

Export goods were conveyed from Japan to other recipients in places even farther away than South or Southeast Asia. As noted above, from an early date lacquer objects traveled either westward or eastward to Europe.[62] It is well known that lacquer objects were prized in early modern European collections, including the *Kunstkammer*. They were also reincorporated into other pieces of furniture. They were even placed

---

[58] See Bhawan Ruangslip, *Dutch East India Company Merchants at the Court of Ayutthaya: Dutch Perceptions of the Thai Kingdom c. 1604–1765* (Leiden and Boston: Brill, 2007).

[59] See the discussion of a box made in Japan about 1650 by Cynthia Viallé in *Asia in Amsterdam*, 113–14 (cat. no. 29).

[60] Impey and Jörg, *Japanese Export Lacquer*, 361–64.

[61] Ibid., 95.

[62] See Impey and Jörg, *Japanese Export Lacquer*, for early trade and collecting in lacquer.

into boiserie as room decorations.[63] This process led to the manufacture of European imitation of lacquer, and to a mania for its collecting and production in the eighteenth century, a subject too broad to touch upon here.

Lacquerware also went to the Americas. When carried by the Portuguese, objects would have been transported to Macao, thence to Malacca, Goa, and on via Africa to Lisbon, whence they may have traveled farther, to Brazil. If by the Spanish, they would have been carried via Manila to New Spain, across the Mexican isthmus, and on to Europe. Many objects sent on to the Americas also stayed there as well as being shipped onwards to Europe. Descriptions and records survive of shipments of lacquerware being sent with destinations in the New World.[64] Goods coming from Portuguese agents until 1640 in Japan or throughout the period from the mid-sixteenth century onwards in Macao could have passed to Europe along the route described above, and then also have been sent via Spain to the Americas. From the 1570s, they could have also have gone via Spanish-ruled Manila to be transported directly across the Pacific Ocean on the 'Manila galleon' to Acapulco in Mexico (New Spain) where they may have remained, as well as being carried across the isthmus to be conveyed to Europe.

Most important, references in inventories indicate the presence of Japanese lacquer-ware objects in collections in Mexico City.[65] Surviving pieces of Japanese lacquer have been discovered in Mexico, where some were employed for unusual purposes. One of the most remarkable cases involves the presence of lacquer in the pilgrimage church of San Miguel

---

[63] See for example Central European contexts *Japanische Lackkunst für Bayerns Fürsten*; Diesinger, *Ostasiatische Lackarbeiten*; Filip Suchomel and Marcela Suchomelová, *A Surface Created for Decoration. Japanese Lacquer Art from the 16th to the 19th Centuries* (Prague: National Gallery, 2002); Martha Boyer, *Japanese Export Lacquers from the Seventeenth Century in the National Museum of Denmark* (Copenhagen: National Museum, 1959); Phillip Herzog von Württemberg, *Das Lackkabinett im deutschen Schlossbau: zur Chinarezeption im 17. und 18. Jahrhundert* (Bern: Peter Lang, 1998); Michael E. Yonan, "Veneers of Authority: Chinese [sic] Lacquers in Maria Theresa' Vienna," *Eighteenth-Century Studies* 37, no. 4 (Summer 2004): 652–72, 702.

[64] See Rodriguez, "Galleon Trade" and Magashima, "Japanese Lacquers."

[65] Sofia Sanabrais, "The *Biombo* or Folding Screen: Examining the Impact of Japan on Artistic Production and the Globalization of Taste in Seventeenth-Century New Spain" (PhD dissertation, New York University, 2005), 133, 299.

de Milagro, in the Mexican state of Tlaxcala east of Mexico City. The pulpit of the church there contains lacquer panels that seem clearly to be of Japanese origin according to their format and pattern. The pulpit is dated by a sculpture on the base 1708. The size, shape, and number (there appear to be six) of these pieces recall the appearance of screens (Japanese *byobu*, Mexican *biombos*).[66] These factors would suggest that a lacquer screen has been inserted, unusually, into a Christian setting.

This remarkable object also points to the impact of Japanese objects in the Americas.[67] Many Japanese folding screens painted in ink on paper or silk were exported to Mexico in numbers. There they are known there as *biombos*, the translation of *byobu*. They engendered a whole mass of New Spanish emulations.[68] Furthermore lacquer objects themselves, both of Chinese and Japanese origins, engendered imitations in Mexico. There a local technique deriving from Pre-Columbian times, wherein an extract from the cochineal insect was used to cover objects, was utilized to create objects and furniture in a European style with both Asian and American motifs[69] (Fig. 3).

A final question remains: how did the lacquer screens come from Japan to Mexico after 1640? As suggested, they must have gone via Manila. But after 1640 Portugal no longer was ruled by Spain, and *nanban* products could not easily have been transported. Neither Spanish nor Portuguese were allowed into Japan. Lacquerware could not have been conveyed directly to the Philippines on Portuguese or Spanish vessels. Lacquer objects would therefore have had to have been transported via the Dutch, but indirectly, since the Dutch were forbidden to travel

---

[66] Sofia Sanabrais, "The *Biombo* or Folding Screen in Colonial Mexico," in *Asia and Spanish America*, 81 and Fig. 7, with arguments for the Japanese origin of the object, 102 n. 94.

[67] See in general Rodrigo Rivero Lake, *Namban Art in Viceregal Mexico* (Madrid: Turner, 2005). The specific subject of lacquer in the Americas, including the kind of object mentioned here, is discussed in Mitchell Codding, "The Lacquer Arts of Latin America," in *Made in the Americas. The New World Discovers Asia*, ed. Dennis Carr (Boston: Museum of Fine Arts, 2015), 75–89.

[68] See Sanabrais, "The *Biombo* or Folding Screen"; further *Viento Detenido. Mitologías e historias en el arte del biombo. Colección de biombos de los siglos XVII al XIX de Museo Soumaya* (Mexico City: Museo Soumaya, 1999).

[69] For an overview see Ruth Lechuga et al., *Lacas Mexicanas* (Mexico City: Museo Franz Mayer, 1997).

Fig. 3 Tray (*Batea*) Mexico, seventeenth century. Lacquered wood with inlaid lacquer decoration, diameter 12 5/16 in. (56.7 cm) Hispanic Society of America LS1978

directly to Spanish-ruled Manila. The Dutch would have brought them to Batavia, whence Chinese Junks would have carried them on to Manila, where Spanish galleons could have brought them to the Americas. Dutch accounts indicate that in fact Chinese junks were much more prevalent than their own ships in the trade with Nagasaki, and that they were also important in the trade to and from the Dutch hub in Batavia. Hence as well as carrying lacquer (both sap and as finished lacquerware) to and from Batavia, Chinese junks could have carried Japanese lacquerware either directly from Japan to Manila, or to Macao, or to Fukien, whence lacquer items would have been brought to Manila.[70] Otherwise lacquer objects might have been traded through the Ryukyuan Islands, which had earlier served as a hub for the Japan-China trade.[71]

Conclusion: Reviewing the Global Question

This chapter has suggested that the Europeans may have played key roles in the worldwide circulation of lacquer materials and finished objects. European insertion in an earlier trade network (like that which had occurred in the Indian Ocean) substantially broadened and altered the extent and content of objects carried in that network. The chain of circumstances demonstrates the Portuguese, their Iberian cousins the Spanish, with whom they were in dynastic union in the crucial years 1580–1640, and the Dutch, their nominal subjects and antagonists, were all involved.

But this essay has also pointed out that the network of circulations was more complex than even a multi-European picture allows.[72] Asians were involved significantly in all the steps of mediation. The Japan trade depended on Chinese, or on Ryukyuan vessels. Moreover, in a number of places whence goods were carried to and from Southeast Asia Chinese merchants were also found along with Dutch.[73] The presence of Chinese junks together with Dutch ships therefore also provides further evidence for the existence of a network of what has recently specifically been called Chinese circulations.[74] This network existed alongside and

---

[70] For the Chinese junk trade and its involvement with the Dutch East India Company, also affecting Dutch trade to and from Japan, see Leonard J. Blussé, "The VOC and the Junk Trade to Batavia," in *Strange Company. Chinese Settlers, Mestizo Women and the Dutch in VOC Batavia* (PhD dissertation, Leiden, Proefschrift; also Dordrecht [as *Verhandelingen, Koninklijk Instituut voor Taal-, Land- en Volkenkunde*, 122), 1986: 97–155; and *idem*, "The Batavia Connection: the Chinese Junks and Their Merchants," and further Miki Sakuraba, "The Chinese Junks; Intermediate Trade Network in Japanese Porcelain for the West," in *Chinese and Japanese Porcelain for the Dutch Golden Age*, 97–108, 109–27.

[71] See Jordan Gschwend, "O Fascínio de Cipango," 198–99.

[72] And eventually the various French, English, Swedish, Danish, and Austrian Netherlandish companies could also have been involved.

[73] See Dijk, *Seventeenth-Century Burma*, Appendix 5.

[74] See *Chinese Circulations. Capital, Commodities and Networks in Southeast Asia*, ed. Eric Tagliacozzo and Wen-Chin Chang (Durham and London: Duke University Press, 2011).

interconnected with European trade circuits, suggesting the existence of other sorts of complex and complicated patterns, whose interaction has also recently received some attention.[75] These interactions correspond, for example, to what historians have otherwise characterized as a process of partnership, or co-colonization.[76] They contribute to the creation of a much more complex picture of European-Asian interrelations in the mediation of art objects and materials in global circulations.

BIBLIOGRAPHY

Andrade, Tonio. 2008. *How Taiwan Became Chinese: Dutch, Spanish, and Han Colonization in the Seventeenth Century*. New York: Columbia University Press.
Arte Namban. Influencia española y portuguesa en el arte japonés siglos xvi y xvii. 1981. Madrid: Museo del Prado.
Beach, Milo Cleveland, and Ebba Koch. 1997. *King of the World. The Padshanama. An Imperial Mughal Manuscript from the Royal Library, Windsor Castle*. London: Azimuth; Washington, DC: Smithsonian Institution.
Biombos Namban/Namban Screens. 2009. Porto: Museu Nacional de Soares dos Reis.
Blussé, Leonard J. 1986. The VOC and the Junk Trade to Batavia. In *Strange Company. Chinese Settlers, Mestizo Women and the Dutch in VOC Batavia*. PhD dissertation, Leiden (Proefschrift; also Dordrecht [as *Verhandelingen, Koninklijk Instituut voor Taal-, Land- en Volkenkunde*, 122), 97–155.
———. 2014. The Batavia Connection: The Chinese Junks and Their Merchants. In *Chinese and Japanese Porcelain for the Dutch Golden Age*, ed. Jan van Campen and Titus Eliëns, 97–108. Zwolle: Waanders.

---

[75] See Kaori Hidaka, "Maritime Trade in Asia and the Circulation of Lacquerware," in *East Asian Lacquer*, and Gabriela Krist and Elfriede Iby, ed., *Investigation and Conservation of East Asian Cabinets in Imperial Residences (1700–1900): Lacquerware & Porcelain. Conference 2013 Postprints* (Vienna: Böhlau, 2015).

[76] Holden Furber, "Asia and the West as Partners Before "Empire" and After," *Journal of Asian Studies* 28 (1969): 711–21; idem, *Rival Empires of Trade in the Orient, 1600–1800* (Minneapolis: University of Minnesota Press, 1976); Tonio Andrade, *How Taiwan Became Chinese: Dutch, Spanish, and Han Colonization in the Seventeenth Century* (New York: Columbia University Press, 2008). The notion of this period being seen as 'The Age of Partnership' has inspired the TANAP series of monographs on the History of Asian-European Interactions: see Leonard Blussé, "Series Editor's Foreword," in Ruangslip, *Dutch East India Company Merchants at the Court of Ayutthaya*, vi.

Blussé, Leonard J., and Felipe Fernández Armesto. 2003. Introduction. In *Shifting Communities and Identity Formation in Early Modern Asia*, ed. Leonard Blussé and Felipe Fernandez Armesto, 2. Leiden: CNWA.

Blussé, Leonard J., M.E. Van Opstall en Ts'ao Yung-ho, with the collaboration of Chiang Shu-sheng and W. Milde (eds.), 1986–2000. *De Dagregisters van het Kasteel Zeelandia, Taiwan, 1629–1662*. The Hague: M. Nijhoff.

Boyer, Martha. 1959. *Japanese Export Lacquers from the Seventeenth Century in the National Museum of Denmark*. Copenhagen: National Museum.

Burke, Peter. 2009. *Cultural Hybridity*. Cambridge, MA: Polity.

Cancela de Abreu, Pedro. 2007. The Construction Techniques of Namban Objects. *After the Barbarians. Namban Works of Art for the Japanese, Portuguese and Dutch Markets*, 52–68. London and Lisbon: Jorge Welsh.

Canepa, Teresa. 2002. Namban Works of Art for the Japanese, Portuguese and Dutch Markets. In *Qing gong shi hui: Yuan cang Riben qi qi te zhan/ Japanese Lacquer from the Ch'ing Court Collection*, ed., Huixia Chen. Taipei: Chu ban.

Clunas, Craig. 2007. *Empire of Great Brightness. Visual and Material Cultures of Ming China, 1368–1644*. London: Reaktion.

Crosby, Alfred W. 1972. *The Columbian Exchange. Biological and Cultural Consequences of 1492*. Westport, CT: Greenwood.

Curvelo, Alexandra. 2007. The Black Ship. In *After the Barbarians. Namban Works of Art for the Japanese, Portuguese and Dutch Markets*, 30–40. London and Lisbon: Jorge Welsh.

———. 2013. Nanban Art: What's Past in Prologue. In *Portugal, Jesuits and Japan. Spiritual Beliefs and Earthly Goods*, ed. Victoria Weston, 76ff. Boston: McMullen Museum of Art, Boston College.

Dagregisters/Diaries Kept by the Heads of the Dutch Factory in Japan. 1974–2007. Tokyo: Daigaku Siryo Hensanjo. 11 vols.

Diesinger, Gunter Rudolf. 1990. *Ostasiatische Lackarbeiten sowie Arbeiten aus Europa, Thailand und Indien*. Braunschweig: Herzog Anton Ulrich-Museum.

Dijk, Wil. O. 2006. *Seventeenth-Century Burma and the Dutch East India Company*. Singapore: NIAS Press.

Erll, Astrid. 2014. Circulating Art and Material Culture: A Model of Transcultural Mediation. In *Mediating Netherlandish Art and Material Culture in Asia*, ed. Thomas DaCosta Kaufmann and Michael North, 321–328. Amsterdam: Amsterdam University Press; Chicago and London: University of Chicago Press.

Finlay, Robert. 2010. *The Pilgrim Art. Cultures of Porcelain in World History*. Berkeley, Los Angeles, and London: University of California Press.

Flores, Jorge, and Nuno Vassallo e Silva (eds.). 2004. *Goa and the Great Mughal*. Lisbon: Calouste Gulbenkian Foundation; London: Scala.

Frank, André Gunder. 1998. *Reorient. Global Economy in the Asian Age*. Berkeley: University of California Press.

Furber, Holden. 1969. Asia and the West as Partners Before "Empire" and After. *Journal of Asian Studies* 28: 711–721.

———. 1976. *Rival Empires of Trade in the Orient, 1600–1800*. Minneapolis: University of Minnesota Press.

Gruzinski, Serge. 2012. *L'aigle et le dragon: Démesure européenne et mondialisation au XVIe siècle*. Paris: Fayard.

———. 2004. *Les Quatre Parties du Monde. Histoire d'une mondialisation*. Paris: La Marinière.

Heginbotham, Arlen, and Michael Schilling. 2011. New Evidence for the Use of Southeast Asian Raw Materials in Seventeenth-Century Japanese Export Lacquer. In *East Asian Lacquer: Material Culture, Science and Conservation*, ed. Shayne Rivers, Rupert Faulkner, and Boris Pretzel, 6–8. London: Victoria and Albert Museum.

Hidaka, Kaori. 2011. Maritime Trade in Asia and the Circulation of Lacquerware. In *East Asian Lacquer: Material Culture, Science and Conservation*, ed. Shayne Rivers, Rupert Faulkner, and Boris Pretzel, 6–8. London: Victoria and Albert Museum.

Honda, Takayuji, Rong Lu, Nobuhiko Kitanto, Yoshimi Kamiya, and Tetsuo Miyakoshi. 2010. Applied Analysis and Identification of Ancient Lacquer Based on Pyrolysis-Gas Chromatography/Mass. *Journal of Applied Polymer Science* 118: 897–901.

Impey, O. P., and C. J. A. Jörg. 2005. *Japanese Export Lacquer 1580–1850*. Amsterdam: Hotei.

Isaacs, Ralph, and T. Richard Blurton. 2000. *Visions from the Golden Land: Burma and the Art of Lacquer*. London: British Museum.

Isaacs, Ralph, Syliva Fantin-lu, Catherine Reymond, and Than Thon U. 2011. *Lacque et or de Birmanie*. Milan: Silvana.

Jordan Gschwend, Annemarie. 1998. O Fascínio de Cipango. Artes Decorativas e lacas da Ásia Oriental em Portugal, Espanha e Áustria (1511–1598). In *Os Construtores do Oriente Português*, 195–223. Porto: Edifico da Alfâmdega.

Jörg, Christiaan J. A. 2007. Dutch VOC Records as a Source for Dating 17th Century Japanese Export Lacquer. In *After the Barbarians. Namban Works of Art for the Japanese, Portuguese and Dutch Markets*, 42–50. London and Lisbon: Jorge Welsh.

Kaufmann, Thomas DaCosta. 1975. Pyxes and Ciboria. In *Eucharistic Vessels of the Middle Ages*, 65–68. Cambridge, MA: Busch-Reisinger Museum; New York: Garland, 1977 (2nd ed.).

Kaufmann, Thomas DaCosta, and Michael North. 2010. Introduction—Artistic and Cultural Exchanges Between Europe and Asia, 1400–1900: Rethinking Markets, Workshops and Collections. In *Artistic and Cultural Exchanges Between Europe and Asia, 1400–1900. Rethinking Markets, Workshops and Collections*, ed. Michael North, 1–8. Farnham and Burlington, VT: Ashgate.

———. 2014. Introduction: Mediating Cultures. In *Mediating Netherlandish Art and Material Culture in Asia*, ed. Thomas DaCosta Kaufmann and Michael North, 7–20. Amsterdam: Amsterdam University Press; Chicago and London: University of Chicago Press.

Kaufmann, Thomas DaCosta, Catherine Dossin, and Béatrice Joyeux-Prunel. 2015. *Circulations in the Global History of Art*. Aldershot and Burlington, VT: Ashgate.

Kitagawa, Miho. 2007. Materials, Tools and Techniques Used on Namban Lacquerwork. In *After the Barbarians. Namban Works of Art for the Japanese, Portuguese and Dutch Markets*, 70–88. London and Lisbon: Jorge Welsh.

Kotani, Noriko. 2010. Studies in Jesuit art in Japan. PhD dissertation, Princeton University.

Krist, Gabriela, and Elfriede Iby (eds.). 2015. *Investigation and Conservation of East Asian Cabinets in Imperial Residences (1700–1900): Lacquerware & Porcelain. Conference 2013 Postprints*. Vienna: Böhlau.

Kühlenthal Michael (ed.). 2000. *Japanische und europäische Lackarbeiten: Rezeption, Adaption, Restaurierung: Deutsch-Japanisches Forschungsprojekt zur Untersuchung und Restaurierung historischer Lacke, gefördert durch das Bundesministerium für Bildung, Wissenschaft, Forschung und Technologie=Japanese and European lacquerware: Adoption, Adaptation, Conservation*. Munich: Bayerisches Landesamt für Denkmalpflege.

Lacas Namban: Huellas de Japón en España: IV Centenario de la Embajada Keichô= Namban Lacquer: Japan remained in Spain: 400 years after the Keicho Embassy. 2013. Madrid: Ministerio de Educación, Cultura y Deporte, Fundación Japón.

Lechuga, Ruth, et. al. 1997. *Lacas Mexicanas*. Mexico City: Museo Franz Mayer.

Levenson, Jay A. (ed.). 2007. *Encompassing the Globe. Portugal and the World in the 16th and 17th Centuries. Reference Catalogue*. Washington, DC: Smithsonian Institution.

Margolin, Jean-Louis, and Claude Markovits. 2015. *Les Indes et L'Europe. Histoires connectées XVe–XXIe siècle*. Paris: Gallimard.

Mendes Pinto, Maria Helena. 1986. *Biombos Namban/Namban Screens*. Lisbon: Museu Nacional de Arte Antiga.

Miyata Rodriguez, Etsuko. 2009. The Early Manila Galleon Trade: Merchants' Networks and Markets in Sixteenth- and Seventeenth-Century Mexico. In *Asia and Spanish America. Trans-Pacific Artistic and Cultural Exchange, 1500–1850*, ed. Donna Pierce and Ronal Otsuka, 37–57. Denver: Denver Art Museum.

Moura Carvalho, Pedro. 2000. Oriental Export Lacquerwares and Their Problematic Origin. In *Exotica Portugals Entdeckungen im Spiegel fürstlicher Kunst-und Wunderkammer der Renaissance (Jahrbuch des kunsthistorischen Museums Wien* 3), ed. Helmut Trnek and Sabine Haag, 246–261.

———. 2008. *Luxury for Export. Artistic Exchange Between India and Portugal around 1600*. Boston: Isabella Stewart Gardner Museum.

———. 2013. The Circulation of European and Asian Works of Art in Japan, circa 1600. In *Portugal, Jesuits and Japan. Spiritual Beliefs and Earthly Goods*, ed. Victoria Weston, 37–43. Boston: McMullen Museum of Art, Boston College.

Nagashima, Meiko. 2009. Japanese Lacquers Exported to Spanish America and Spain. In *Asia and Spanish America. Trans-Pacific Artistic and Cultural Exchange, 1500–1850*, ed. Pierce, Donna, and Ronal Otsuka, 107–117. Denver: Denver Art Museum.

Nelson, John. 2002. Myths, Missions, and Mistrust. The Fate of Christianity in Sixteenth and Seventeenth Century Japan. *History and Anthropology* 13 (2): 93–111.

Osswald, Cristina. 2013. *Written in Stone. Jesuit Buildings in Goa and Their Artistic and Architectural Features*. Goa: Goa 1556 and Golden Heart Emporium Bookshop.

Pierce, Donna, and Ronal Otsuka. 2009. *Asia and Spanish America. Trans-Pacific Artistic and Cultural Exchange, 1500–1850*. Denver: Denver Art Museum.

Rivero Lake, Rodrigo. 2005. *Namban Art in Viceregal Mexico*. Madrid: Turner.

Ruangslip, Bhawan. 2007. *Dutch East India Company Merchants at the Court of Ayutthaya. Dutch Perceptions of the Thai Kingdom c. 1604–1765*. Leiden and Boston: Brill.

Sakuraba, Miki. 2014. The Chinese Junks; Intermediate Trade Network in Japanese Porcelain for the West. In *Chinese and Japanese Porcelain for the Dutch Golden Age*, ed. Jan van Campen and Titus Eliëns, 109–127. Zwolle: Waanders.

Sanabrais, Sofia. 2005. The Biombo or Folding Screen: Examining the Impact of Japan on Artistic Production and the Globalization of Taste in Seventeenth-Century New Spain. PhD dissertation, New York University.

Sanabrais, Sofia. 2009. The Biombo or Folding Screen in Colonial Mexico. In *Asia and Spanish America. Trans-Pacific Artistic and Cultural Exchange, 1500–1850*, ed. Donna Pierce and Ronal Otsuka. Denver: Denver Art Museum.

Suchomel, Filip, and Marcela Suchomelová. 2002. *A Surface Created for Decoration. Japanese Lacquer Art from the 16th to the 19th Centuries*. Prague: National Gallery.

Tagliacozzo, Eric, and Wen-Chin Chang (eds.). 2011. *Chinese Circulations. Capital, Commodities and Networks in Southeast Asia*. Durham and London: Duke University Press.

Varela Gomes, Paulo. 2011. *Whitewash, Redstone. A History of Church Architecture in Goa*. New Delhi: Yoda Press.

van Campen, Jan, and Titus Eliëns (eds.). 2014. *Chinese and Japanese Porcelain for the Dutch Golden Age*. Zwolle: Waanders.

Vassallo e Silva, Nuno. 2010. A Companhia de Jesus e as artes decorativas no Oriente português. In *Arte Oriental nas Colecções do Museu de São*. 21, Fig. 5 and 6. Roque. Lisbon: Santa Casa da Misericórdia.

Viallé, Cynthia. 2010. Fit for Kings and Princes: A Gift of Japanese Lacquer. In *Large and Broad. The Dutch Impact on Early Modern Asia. Essays in Honor of Leonard Blussé*, ed. Nagazumi Yōko, 188–222. Tokyo: The Toyo Bunko.

———. 2011. Japanese Lacquer Cabinets in the Records of the Dutch East India Company. In *Japanische Lackkunst für Bayerns Fürsten. Die Japanischen Lackmöbel der Staatlichen Münzsammlung*, ed. Anton Schweizer et. al., 31–46. Munich: Staatlichen Münzsammlung.

———. 2011. Two Boxes and Two Balustrades; Private Orders for Fine Japanese Export Lacquer. In *East Asian Lacquer: Material Culture, Science and Conservation*, ed. Shayne Rivers, Rupert Faulkner, and Boris Pretzel. London: Victoria and Albert Museum and Archetype.

Viento Detenido. Mitologías e historias en el arte del biombo. Colección de biombos de los siglos XVII al XIX de Museo Soumaya. 1999. Mexico City: Museo Soumaya.

Watt, James C. Y., and Barbara B. Ford. 1991. *East Asian Lacquer, the Florence and Herbert Irving Collection*. New York: Metropolitan Museum of Art.

Weigelt, Uta. 2005. *Birmas Lackkunst in deutschen Museen*. Münster: Museum für Lackkunst.

Württemberg, Phillip Herzog von. 1998. *Das Lackkabinett im deutschen Schlossbau: zur Chinarezeption im 17. und 18. Jahrhundert*. Bern: Peter Lang.

Yonan, Michael E. 2004. Veneers of Authority: Chinese [sic] Lacquers in Maria Theresa' Vienna. *Eighteenth-Century Studies* 37 (4) (Summer): 652–672, 702.

Paradise in Stone: Representations of New World Plants and Animals on Spanish Colonial Churches in the Philippines

Raquel A. G. Reyes

Abstract Trade in the plants and animals of the New World exerted a profound influence on the imaginations of Filipino architects and stonemasons. Eighteenth-century church façades, designed and wrought by Filipino maestros de obras, are distinguished for their elaborate ornamentation and sensuous depictions of the natural world. Scholars have commented on the luxurious and extravagant detailing of the stonework, but have yet to examine the context of commercial exchanges and cultural innovation in which imported trees, fruit, flowers, and animals such as horses were chosen to embellish church walls. Focusing on several examples, notably the baroque, fortress-like church at Miag-ao in Iloilo, the western Visayas, I shall explore the botanical and animal stone imagery as a striking architectural innovation and expressions of local aesthetics, as evidence of local interest in exotic naturalia, and as an ebullient celebration of the flora and fauna that had come to the archipelago from the New World.

R. A. G. Reyes (✉)
Department of History, School of Oriental and African Studies,
University of London, London, UK

Keywords Philippines · Spanish colonialism · Galleon trade · Church architecture and façades · New World plants and animals · Rococo

Introduction

The façade can be the most ornamented part of a church's exterior. Its dramatic monumentality seeks to instruct, awe, and inspire. Carvings of flowers, vines, plants, foliage, and stylized renderings of fruits and animals ornament the stone façades and interior features of some Spanish-era colonial churches found in the main Philippine islands of Luzon and the Visayas. Distinguished by their flowing, wavy lines, exuberant vitality, and rich artistic details, these strikingly elaborate surface decorations and embellishments have long been regarded as representative of 'Filipino Baroque' and 'Filipino Rococo' styles.

The incorporation of New World flora and fauna is a spectacular highlight of this ornate decoration. Fruits from the Americas, notably pineapple, papaya, and guava, and animals, such as horses, are extravagant and luxurious details that have been interpreted as expressions of native originality and imagination. Viewed as evidence of the involvement of indigenous sculptors and artisans, these ornamentations have been said to mark Spanish colonial religious architecture with a distinctively Filipino artistic style. Yet fruits and animals from the New World were initially foreign things in the everyday life of the general populace. How can we best understand their incorporation and presence on colonial church architecture?

Since the late 1940s, nationalist perspectives in Philippine history have played a vital role in nation building and continue to generate heated scholarly debates.[1] A common thread running through this literature is the effort to identify, define, and apprehend so-called 'Filipino' elements within European or Spanish architectural style—what those elements might mean, their nature, appearance, and modes of practice which signal difference between native Filipino, European/Spanish, and other foreign cultural forms and practices.[2]

---

[1] See, for instance, Guillermo (2001), Flores (1998), Perez (1989), and Hila (1992).

[2] Philippine scholarship has largely focused on descriptive analyses and liturgical significance. Major works are Trota José (1991), *Of War and Peace* (2009), *Endangered Fil-Hispanic Architecture* (2005), Javellana (1997), *Wood and Stone* (1991), Spinola (1959), Galende (1987), and Coseteng (1972).

Spanish-era colonial churches in the Philippines generally lack uniformity in surface design and embody Castilian/European, Latin American, Islamic, and Chinese architectural styles and features. What native peoples brought into this mix remains an intriguing interpretive conundrum. Writing in 1951, the Hungarian-American art historian Pal Kelemen observed that:

> Spanish Baroque spread through the islands, but it was much modified... Native building methods introduced change, as did also the use of wood, cane, thatch, and other tropical materials. Tropical flora furnished new motifs to be ornately carved in stone. The sumptuous church interiors were decorated with treasures, many of them brought from China and Japan, so that local artisans could draw for inspiration not only on their own land and on Europe, but also on their Oriental neighbors.[3]

These remarks proved to be a touchstone for Filipino art historians who had become familiar with colonial art of the Americas and had sought to find analogous examples in the Philippines. The eminent Filipino scholar, Benito Legarda Jr., has suggested four areas in which indigeneity may be recognized in Philippine art and architecture: first, the involvement of native labor and artisanal skill in the use of local materials; second, the local origins of motifs; third, the 'blending' or 'inter-cultural fusion' of indigenous elements with those of Spanish, Latin American, Chinese, and other foreign styles; and fourth, the localization of specific objects or things that, although were not wrought by native hands, nonetheless came to embody 'a combination of artistic elements which can be found only in the Philippines'.[4]

Legarda based his observations on a survey of colonial churches in the Ilocos region, along coastal northwest Luzon, a geographic area with an arid climate and poor soil. Colonial Ilocano churches are made of brick, coral, and river rock. They notably lack uniformity of design, despite the evangelization of the area by a single religious order, the Augustinians. Façades of these churches, Legarda writes eloquently, are generally characterized by 'simplicity, sincerity, straightforwardness, and strength' and exhibit a hybrid nature that contains 'native modifications of foreign elements, native combinations of such elements, as well as some native elements themselves'. In the type of façade he identifies

---

[3] Kelemen (1951: 74).
[4] Legarda (1960).

as 'Ilocano Baroque' for instance, he discerns a style that is lacking in sophisticated ornamentation, though possessing certain prominent features of which are 'the decorative use of columns or piers against the wall without pediments, and the presence of numerous finials shaped like urns, knobs or pyramids', amounting to 'rude charm and folk attractiveness'.[5] Regional styles, he concludes, emerged from the exigencies of geography, and distinct ethno-linguistic and diocesan divisions.

Just over twenty years later, Legarda's survey of the churches in an adjoining region, the Cagayan Valley, an area controlled by the Dominican order, offers a further illustrative case study of the idea that church-building styles evolved from defined regions. The 'Cagayan style', Legarda observes, constituted structures made predominately from brick and the following features: flying buttresses, spiral or Solomonic columns, and pertinently, ornamental façades. In particular, attention is drawn to clay insets 'in the form of rosettes, cornucopiae, festoons, sun faces, angel faces, floral and foliate forms, animal and human figures, as well as religious symbols and coats of arms'.[6] The late eighteenth-century church at Dupax possesses walls elaborately decorated with vines and leaves; at Angadanan Viejo, there are grooved columns crowned by brick and clay shapes resembling cones or pineapples; and at Tumauini, dated from 1783 to 1788, which Legarda refers to as the 'supreme achievement of the Cagayan region, the jewel of the Valley', the church most exemplifying the style, the clay insets are heavily ornamented with floral designs among other elements, and the cylindrical bell tower, dated from the early nineteenth century, features garlands and figures of birds.[7] Interestingly, for our purpose although Legarda makes only passing mention, the outburst of church-building activity coincided with vigorous economic and agricultural activities—the cultivation of New World produce such as potatoes and string beans, plantations, and the establishment of the tobacco monopoly.[8]

Today, there is an impressive corpus of work documenting the architecture and internal features of Spanish-era churches in the Philippines. Scholars who have written about 'Filipino-ness' in church architecture

---

[5] Legarda (1960: 15–140).
[6] Legarda (1981: 72–75).
[7] Legarda (1981: 75); see also Galván (2001: 294).
[8] De Jesus (1998).

have debated considerations of geography, climate, functionality, and the levels and limitations of technical knowledge.

The popular term 'earthquake Baroque' is applied to the architectural forms whose beginnings were determined by improvisation and a pragmatic fear of the tremblor. Massive, disproportionate-sized buttresses and immensely thick walls serving to withstand the ravages of fire, quake, and the attack of raiders and hostile military forces, figured into the commonplace two-storied rectangular structures, a triangular pediment, drastically reduced fenestrations, relatively low ceilings, and a single, long nave.[9] Moreover, Fernando Nakpil Zialcita has observed how Filipino construction finds expression in relation to a sense of space, movement, and feeling. Where Zialcita sees '...tension, drama, and vertical striving' in the architecture of Spanish and Mexican churches, Filipino churches are, in contrast, 'spread out and relaxed', their oversized buttresses 'reinforce a sense of breadth rather than height', and the absence of vaulted ceilings 'communicate a lightness of feeling' which corresponds with the 'Filipino temperament which seems more lyrical than dramatic'.[10] In this interpretation, local structures that appear to be schematized and slavish to foreign concepts of space and proportion are, instead, shown to be unique adaptations that developed in response to environmental conditions, particular needs, and a purported indigenous personality. More emphatically, ornamental elaboration and embellishment have been attributed to native disposition—an intrinsic inclination for embellishment, or, as René Javellana has put it, a 'horror vacui...the fear of empty spaces'. It has also been speculated that a transfer of skills from one medium to another may have occurred. Since stone carving lacks a history in Philippine plastic arts, the skill and ingenuity applied to ornate surface decorations rendered in stone could trace its evolutionary origins to the more ancient traditions of woodworking and weaving.[11]

This chapter will emphasize material interactions arising, in particular, from the early modern galleon trade and the cultural and commercial exchanges it facilitated. Churches in the southern Luzon and Visayas regions of the Philippines are here explored with the aim of understanding artistic depictions of New World flora and fauna through a historical

---

[9] Javellana (1997) and Trota José (1991: 51–53).
[10] Zialcita (2005: 205).
[11] Smith (1958: 1–10) and Javellana et al. (1997, cited in Invernizzi Tettoni 1997).

materialist lens. How were these artistic representations influenced by material conditions, such as geographic location, connections to trading networks and local industries, the availability of local labor and materials, the impact of American edible plants on local diets, and the religious-didactic purposes of the designs? We shall return later to the question of 'Filipino style', and which elements of church architecture might be seen as evidence of indigenous agency.

Manila-Acapulco Galleon Trade

In 1564, the Spanish Crown instructed the conquistador Miguel López de Legazpi (1501–1572) to launch an expedition to the Philippine Islands. Motivated primarily by the desire to gain a foothold in the Southeast Asian spice trade, then dominated by the Portuguese, Legazpi was ordered to bring back samples of spices and discover a return route to New Spain. His expedition arrived in the central Visayas in 1565 and was initially disappointed, finding little in the way of spices and gold for profit. After a six-year sojourn on the island of Cebu, the expedition transferred to the lowlands of Luzon, establishing a permanent base at a settlement known as 'Maynilad'. Legazpi had found a sheltered natural harbor on the eastern side of a bay and at the mouth of the Pasig River. There the expedition encountered a small, scattered population of natives, settlers, merchants, and Muslim missionaries. Legazpi learned that the Muslim missionaries and native converts nurtured commercial and cultural ties with neighboring Muslim centers spanning the Jolo archipelago in southern Philippines, Borneo, Aceh, at the northern tip of Sumatra, the Moluccas, within the Indonesian archipelago, Malacca in the Malay Peninsula, and Pattani in the southern region of Thailand. At various times of the year, Chinese merchants arrived in trading junks laden with wares to do business with the coastal Malays, who favored their jars and dishes. Attracted by its safe harbor, its strategic position that allowed for intra-regional trade, and its entrenched Sino-Filipino-Muslim trade networks, Legazpi instituted Manila as the capital of the Philippine archipelago in 1571.

Seven years earlier, the circumnavigator and Augustinian friar Andrés de Urdaneta (1498–1568) had sailed northeasterly from the island of Cebu and, climbing between thirty-seven and thirty-nine degrees, his ship caught the prevailing westerlies across the Pacific, skirted the California coast, and reached Acapulco with a total journey time of four months. The discovery of this fast and efficient return route across the Pacific to Mexico was critical to the commercial success of the Spanish colonial enterprise in the Pacific. The trans-Pacific galleon trade began almost immediately, with the first of the mighty 'Manila galleons' sailing for Acapulco in 1571, the last in 1815.[12] Departing from Manila, the galleons annually set forth westward to Acapulco bringing Chinese silks, spices, precious metals, perfumes, foodstuffs, and other luxuries from the East and then returned loaded with silver from Spanish America that was desired by China. Neither demand outweighed the other. The galleons were the richest ships in the world, and with the trans-Pacific trade, Spain came to dominate commerce with America and Europe in both silk and spices. The significance of this demand and supply commerce, and the route taken to facilitate it, was far-reaching. Through the lucrative trade, Manila was transformed into the colony's preeminent political, religious, multiracial, trading hub, and one of the wealthiest and greatest commercial entrepôts in Asia. Not only did two world regions come into contact with one another for the first time through the direct exchange of goods, but the trade influenced the histories of four continents—Europe, the Americas, Asia, and Africa.[13]

Agriculture and everyday diets were immeasurably enriched by the migration of crops and animals[14]: wheat, cattle, and horses traveled from the Old World to the New World, while New World potatoes, tomatoes, paprika went to Europe, maize and cassava to Africa, maize, sweet potatoes, and tomatoes to Asia. In maritime Southeast Asia, maize and sweet potato spread rapidly and widely to become prominent staples. In certain areas especially vulnerable to unseasonable weather, they even supplanted the traditional staples of indigenous millet, and roots and tubers, specifically aroids and yams, the most important being taro (*Colocasi esculenta*) and ube (*Dioscorea hispida*), respectively.[15]

---

[12] Although the galleon trade ended in 1815, the Acapulco trade continued until Mexican independence in 1821 on ships that were not galleons (Legarda 1999).

[13] Flynn et al. (2001), Spate (1979), Flynn et al. (1999), Tremml-Werner (2015), Giraldez (2015), and Reyes (2017). On slavery and the Trans-Pacific trade, see Seijas (2014).

[14] Much has been written about the global movement of plants and animals after 1492, a process that has come to be famously known as the Columbian Exchange, and how this brought about profound environmental changes. See the seminal work by Crosby (1972).

[15] Boomgaard and 't Hart (2010), Boomgaard (1999), and Boomgaard (2003b).

The Manila–Acapulco voyages facilitated important botanical exchanges. Coconuts from the Philippines taken aboard Manila galleons were responsible for the introduction and spread of modern coconut populations in Mexico and southward to Peru.[16] The return voyages brought cereals and beans, fruiting trees, peanuts and pineapple, medicinals, ornamentals, and textile plants.[17] Aromatic flavorings such as vanilla reached the Philippines, possibly from Guatemala or El Salvador[18]; tobacco was planted as a crop as early as 1575; spices, including five different species of chilli peppers, diffused from the Philippines to the Fujian and Zhejiang Provinces in China by the late seventeenth century. Indicative of their local acceptance, chilli peppers came to be known collectively by the vernacular term *buyobuyo*,[19] the Visayan word for the widespread and common betel leaf, areca nut, and lime masticatory. Chocolate (*Theobroma cacao*), as the chapter by William G. Clarence-Smith in this volume shows, was favored primarily by the Spanish Catholic clergy as a hot beverage, but was soon enthusiastically adopted by elites. Galleon shipments of New World cattle were accommodated on arable lands that were given over to ranches and livestock-raising. Used to provision the galleons, *rancherias* or cattle ranches were 'an instance of geographical influence stemming from the needs of the trans-pacific trade'.[20] Horses were brought first from Mexico and quickly flourished. By the late seventeenth century, foreigners noted their plentiful presence in Luzon and Mindanao where, latterly, feral herds roamed.[21]

The influences of Hispanic gastronomy and its penetration of indigenous culinary life, particularly within elite society, and the indigenization of Hispanic foods, are evident in linguistic assimilations, the introduction of new cookery methods, gastronomic exchanges, and culinary adaptations. Rafael Bernal has pointed to the names of foods of Mexican origin that entered the local lexicon. Examples are legion—*achuete* or *atsuete* from achiote or annatto (*Bixa orellana*), the seeds from which red food

[16] Harris (2012).
[17] Alvina and Madulid (2009: 11).
[18] Lubinsky et al. (2008).
[19] Smith (2015: 73–74).
[20] Guzman-Rivas (1960: 175).
[21] Bankoff (2004: 233).

coloring is obtained, *panocha* for the brown, unrefined, coarse-grained sugar, papaya, *casaba* or cassava, *aguacate/abokado* or avocado, just to name a few.[22] Hispanic food came to be associated with wealthy, urbanized, lifestyles—luxurious, classy, and expensive food of the rich. The use of certain ingredients that were heavy on the stomach and rich in taste, such as beef and cured pork meat, contrasted sharply with the native fare of fish and vegetables, and demanded new cooking methods—sautéing or *guisar* and frying in oils, *prito*.[23]

THE PINEAPPLE

Some New World plants found uses other than as edibles. Brought on the galleons, pineapples prevented sailors from falling ill from scurvy on the long voyage. The fruit was transplanted and successfully cultivated in the Visayas, where artisans skilled at weaving fabric from plant fibers, most commonly from *Musa textilis*, a species of banana, which produced *sinamay*, soft, fine cloth, and *abaca* or hemp for strong cordage, found pineapple leafstalks just as useful. *Piña* cloth, a light, luxurious, diaphanous material, was laborious to produce and hence expensive, but soon found favor among the elite. Spanish missionaries in Lumban, in the Laguna province in southern Luzon, encouraged local artisans to overlay plain *piña* cloth woven in Aklan, Iloilo, and Pan-ay in the Visayas, with intricate embroidery, a skill they had learned from emigrant Chinese, thus tripling the price. Used for women's blouses, the *baro* and *camisa*, shawl collars, *pañuelo*, and skirts, *saya*, demand for the embroidered cloth rose exponentially in the eighteenth century. Gifted to European royalty on occasions such as weddings and coronations, *piña* cloth was a high-value and prestigious textile, signifying the high social status of the wearer. By the mid-nineteenth century, it had become an important export commodity competing with European lace in the international market.[24]

The pineapple appears as a decorative motif in several places—notably in Manila's San Agustin Church and at Pan-ay Church on the island of Pan-ay in the western Visayas. The motif traces a connection to prosperity

---

[22] Bernal (1965).
[23] Fernandez and Alegre (1988: 150). For an indication of the enduring Hispanic culinary legacy, see David-Perez (1973).
[24] Montinola (1991) and Milgram (2009).

and the textile trade. In San Agustin Church, an inverted pineapple appears as a fabulous detail on a magnificently carved and embellished pulpit. Built in 1604, part of a building boom that had transformed Manila since its founding in 1571, San Agustin is externally formal, solid, and austere. Its façade, with the exception of elaborately carved wooden main doors, is plain. However, the interiors are richly decorated and complex: The single nave configuration is flanked by long, 'deep', so-called crypto-collateral chapels reminiscent of churches in Mexico; ovoid stone arches extended across the width of the nave and led the eye toward a soaring barrel-vaulted ceiling, an ornate choir stall and gilded retablos.[25]

The literature is uncertain when and by whom the pulpit was carved, although it seems to have been commissioned in 1627. Other interior features of the church may provide some clues. San Agustin's gilded retablo, richly carved with niches bearing saints, was installed in 1617 or 1618 and carved by a silversmith named Juan de los Santos who was the *sacristan mayor* of San Pablo, a small town in the Laguna province. Whether he was of Chinese ethnicity or a native is not clear. He is known to have been the creator of a processional monstrance, an elaborately decorated vessel wrought in precious metals in which an object of piety is displayed, and he may have been responsible for carving a large ivory crucifix.[26] The pulpit was possibly also executed by Juan de los Santos, whose skills were evidently highly regarded enough for him to be sent from Laguna on important commissions.

In the Visayas, the Augustinian church in Pan-ay is adorned with pineapple-shaped finials on the pediment walls (Fig. 1). The foundations of the church can be traced to between 1692 and 1698, but after being damaged by several fires, the church was rebuilt using coral stones in 1774 by Fray Manuel Murguia. His opulent Baroque tastes found expression in marble flooring, extravagantly decorated and gilded hardwood retablos, bas-reliefs and religious statuary executed by the town's Indio sculptor, Joséph Bergaño or *Sarhento Itak*, who was also responsible for carving the finials.[27] Pan-ay then was an integral part of an established network of intra-regional trade and had shifted from a subsistence

---

[25] Coseteng (1972: 52–53).
[26] Trota José (1990: 20).
[27] Galende (1987: 319).

Fig. 1   Pan-ay Church, pineapple-shaped finials (Photo by Author)

economy to commercial textile production. In particular, *sinamay* fine abaca fabric, *abaca* and *piña* textiles, woven from the fibers of wild banana (*musa textilis*) and pineapple leaves, mixed with cotton and silk, were commanding fabulous prices in Europe and bringing significant wealth to the town.[28] It seems likely that pineapple-shaped finials were not simply added for 'exotic' interest, and that their inclusion was closely associated with the highly profitable *piña* textile industry and paid tribute to a commerce that significantly benefited the island's inhabitants.[29]

Pineapple motifs functioned symbolically on several levels. The fruit was (and is still) regarded by the Chinese as a sign of hospitality, luck, and good fortune, and some scholars take its presence in church embellishments to indicate the hand of Chinese artisans.[30] It is possible, too, that the motif was a reformulation of the pinecone, a well-known Euro-Christian Catholic symbol for eternal life, for local usage, thus possessing

[28] McCoy (1982).
[29] Galende (1987: 321).
[30] Galende (1987: 242).

educational value.[31] Highly decorative retablos featuring carvings and reliefs of religious symbols, medallions, and seals of the friar orders, sculptures of saints, paintings, liturgical vessels and ornaments such as chalices and reliquaries, were costly additions to churches but they were also devotional objects, and taught early Filipino converts about the faith, and familiarized them with Christian values and duties.[32] Pan-ay Church features shallow coupled pilasters and niches bearing statues of Augustinian saints, embellishments which would have worked as visual aids in teaching converts about Augustinian theology. That said, though, it is possible too that didactic purposes went some way toward legitimating the acquisition of treasures and justifying architectural ornamentation of churches and the opulence of their interiors.

Filipinos and Spaniards alike favored showy church interiors; they shared a taste for the lavish. But church embellishments and ornamentation were costly, fundamentally depending upon the wealth of a parish and the availability of skilled labor. Manila and Pan-ay fulfilled both these conditions. The pineapple motif was an emblem of prosperity. Its presence signaled a further triumph—the crossover success of a New World fruit.

Church Building and Commerce

Soon after their arrival in the Philippines, the Spanish mendicant orders—the Augustinians (from 1565 onwards), Franciscans (1577), Dominicans (1587), Recollects (1606) and Jesuits (1581) and the secular clergy set about organizing and grouping the largely scattered native settlements into communities known as *reducciones*. The rationale behind this arrangement was simple enough: getting the freshly colonized natives to live in the vicinity of the church bell—*bajo la campana*—facilitated their control, administration, and Christian conversion. Spanish missionaries swiftly established parishes in and around Manila, notably Tondo and Binondo, Santa Ana, San Pedro Makati, and other villages up the Pasig River; they fanned out beyond the environs of Manila to Taal in Batangas and to several towns along the shores of Laguna de Bay and into the hills of Laguna province. With the arrival

---

[31] Impelluso (2004).
[32] Trota José (1991: 74).

of the Jesuits, mission towns such as San Mateo, Antipolo, Taytay, and Tanay were established east of Manila in the Marikina Valley and on the slopes of the Sierra Madre.

The Tagalog-speaking lowlanders of this southern Luzon region farmed, fished, and practiced wet-rice cultivation. Conquest and missionization bound the area to the fortunes of Manila and the friar orders. Forty percent of the land in the environs of Manila—Tondo, Cavite, Bulacan and Laguna de Bay—was owned by the religious orders. Friar estates were vast, swallowing up communal lands and effectively turning the native populace into tenant farmers and laborers of haciendas that undertook the commercial provisioning of the colonial capital. The monumental stone churches and plazas of Manila's Intramuros—structures that were heavily fortified and enclosed by thick, defensive walls—were direct beneficiaries of this system of food and labor provisioning.

In the upland areas, church façades were eclectic. Towns on the mountain slopes and near the rivers of southern Luzon produced some of the most ornate churches in the country. In the province of Laguna, notably in the hilly areas where Franciscans evangelized, church façades are visually flamboyant and burst with floral detail. Paete Church, for example, first built in 1646 and rebuilt in 1717, is distinguished by bas-reliefs of intricately entwining floral and acanthus leaves. A relief of St James on horseback trampling on the bodies of Moors provides a focal point (Fig. 2). Scholars have attributed this masterful stonework to native craftsmen and the woodworking tradition of Paete, 'a town where the ancient occupation of wood carving had infused itself locally and artistically'.[33] Paete had an enduring influence on the ornamentation of other churches in the region. Morong church, distantly reminiscent of Italian Baroque, and built in 1615 under the direction of Chinese master craftsmen, benefited later, in the mid-nineteenth century, from the wood-carving expertise of Don Bartolome Palatino from Paete. In nearby Pakil, a *visita*, that is, a hamlet without its own priest, of Paete founded in 1676, a church built in the mid-eighteenth century is richly decorated with florid stone appliques and floral decoration, and whimsical details such as winged cherub heads, saints' medallions, and ornamented frames around niches. This stylized floral decoration appears on a smaller scale in Taal, in nearby Batangas province, on a reef-stone arch

---

[33] Coseteng (1972: 123).

Fig. 2 Paete Church, detail showing St James on horse-back (Photo by Author)

over a natural spring well referred to as the *balon Santa Lucia*, close to the banks of the Pansipit River. The spring is believed to be the site of a Marian apparition, known locally as the Virgin of Caysasay. The arch possibly dates to around the mid-eighteenth century.[34] It is decorated with urns carved in high relief, from which emerge acanthus leaves like gushes of spring water.

Defensive or strategic purposes often dictated the locations of churches. But elevated inland positions, particularly at points near or commanding views of both mountain, forests, natural springs, and rivers, such as the churches at Paete and Pakil, may have connected to other ancient beliefs and deep-seated cultural motivations. Throughout Southeast Asia, mountains were believed to be holy and were often recognized as supreme deities that possessed a life-giving force. In the form of volcanoes, mountains were life-threatening entities, with the power to unleash death and destruction. They could also be sacred places where ancestral spirits dwelled, or, as evidenced by the Islamic tombs and

[34] Trota José (2002: 112).

mosques found on mountaintops in Java, as sanctuaries of saints. Springs, according to the Balinese, were places in which the gods bathed and spring water, used for ritualistic purposes, was thought to be purifying, fertilizing, and life-enhancing.[35] It is perhaps no coincidence that the elaborate ornamentation of Pakil church is stylistically similar to Taal's *balon de Sta. Lucia* and also lies close to a natural spring where a Marian devotion, known as Our Lady of Sorrows of Turumba, emerged in the eighteenth century. Beyond Laguna and further south, the early nineteenth-century Franciscan church in the town of Daraga in the Bicol region is situated on a mountaintop with a view of Mayon Volcano. It is considered one of the best examples of so-called indigenous Baroque. The façade, attributed to native craftsmen, features four solomonic pillars with spiraling grooves filled with twisting vines bearing clusters of grapes, and a 'riotous display' of floral ornamentation expressing a free-wheeling, extravagant, and imaginative temperament.

The stucco technique of stone carving was used in all these examples. This method coats the surface of the façade with a thin plaster of stucco, *paletada*, onto which reliefs are carved. The stucco protected the stone and brick from the elements and resulted in reliefs that were visually bold yet soft in effect.[36] Ingredients for mortar that bound together the stones and bricks varied from mixtures of sand, lime, and plant sap, to the inclusion of egg shells and egg whites. Lime came from limestone, coral, or small shells, the latter was crushed and *piedra buga*, pumice, added. The vast quantities of egg whites that are known to have been used in some churches have led church historian Regalado Trota José to speculate whether this helped popularize the Hispanic egg yolk-rich desserts *leche flan, tocino del cielo*, and *yema*.[37]

These sorts of artistic and constructional innovations required considerable financing and labor. In theory, the friar orders lived a sequestered life in priories, monasteries or *conventos*, took a vow of poverty, and survived on alms and charity. In contrast, secular priests ministered to a specific area or diocese and lived among their parishioners with whom they freely mixed. They were permitted to accept benefices and legacies left

---

[35] Boomgaard (2003a) and Christie (1992). Other than studies of Mount Banahaw cults, little scholarly attention has been given to churches and Marian shrines in the upland areas of Laguna.

[36] Trota José (1991: 38).

[37] Ibid.

to them by donors in exchange for masses and prayers for the donor and family. These bequests could mean a fixed income and were sometimes generous enough to maintain a priest to a comfortable standard and hence were actively sought out.[38] In practice, charity represented only one source of income.

As in the Americas, the religious orders in the Philippines became deeply enmeshed in the colonial economy. Nicholas Cushner and, more recently, Barbara Andaya have highlighted the commercial activities of clergy in Southeast Asia, drawing attention to the combination of factors that compelled clerical involvement in trade. Priests extracted ecclesiastical tribute from their parishioners who were obliged to recompense them for their services. Parishioners provided resources, from food to labor, *gratis*, to the clergy. Even when locals could sell their products, there was an ever-present pressure to do so for far less than the market value.[39] Tribute demands, *vandalas* or forced sales, and the *polo* or forced labor, exerted by the Spanish authorities could be harshly oppressive on the native population. According to Linda Newson, major population decline occurred during the Hispano-Dutch War from 1604 to 1648 and in periods of intense construction—the construction of Manila's urban infrastructure, churches and fortifications, galleon, and military ships is a case in point. Tribute levies were usually both in cash and in kind: Rice, chickens, eggs, and pigs were the most common requisitioned agricultural products. As the sixteenth century drew to a close, exactions in the region considerably increased: Each month, the *alcalde mayores* were reportedly ordered to supply 300 egg-laying hens, 2000 eggs, and as many pigs.[40] While quotas were set, these were often exceeded, causing hardship on farmers who were unable to meet their quotas, forcing them into debt or to flee from their homes. *Polo* labor ers were seldom paid wages and endured difficult conditions and poor food rations, especially in the shipyards, and many evaded conscription by fleeing.[41]

Encomiendas were 'areas of jurisdiction', usually encompassing several villages and surrounding countryside, commended by the Spanish

---

[38] Javellana (2010: 33).
[39] Cushner (1971) and Andaya (2009).
[40] Newson (2009: 141).
[41] Newson (2009).

Crown to the care of a conquistador who would then become known as the *encomendero* of that locality. According to the Filipino Jesuit historian Horacio de la Costa, the encomendero was obliged to maintain law and order, protect the people from their enemies, come to their aid in their necessities, and instruct them in the Catholic faith. In exchange, they had the right to extract tribute and statute labor from the number of natives allocated to them.[42] Within this system, the cost of building a church was shared between the encomendero, the government, and the tribute paying community, the latter being largely responsible for the heavy construction work.[43] If the town was large enough, then the native community shouldered the entire cost and labor, which involved quarrying stones, the extraction and hewing of timber, and making bricks and lime. This was an extremely onerous burden for the population and often encouraged fugitivism. The construction of the massive mid-seventeenth-century church in Majayjay, Laguna, complete with enormous buttresses or *contrafuertes*, took two slow and painful decades of statute labor, tributes, fines, and floggings. The majority of the town's inhabitants simply fled. From 1711 to 1730, there was a push to reconstruct the church that had by this time fallen into ruin. Again, the population was resistant to provide labor. The monumental structure that resulted has been described as having a 'primitive quality'.[44] Throughout the nineteenth century, the church sustained heavy damage, not from earthquakes but from a succession of typhoons.

Although considered unseemly among the more high-minded members of the clergy and officially frowned upon, clerical participation in the galleon trade was enthusiastic. From the beginning, religious and secular priests enjoyed the same advantages and privileges as other Spanish traders. The Ecclesiastical Cabildo of Manila, composed of priests, was a trading bloc ostensibly formed to augment clerical incomes but, in practice, there seemed to be no way of telling whether it was real financial need or the amassing of capital in the name of profit that lay behind clerical motivations.[45] The economic interests of the Jesuits found graphic expression in a map by the Jesuit Father Pedro Murillo Velarde

---

[42] De la Costa (1961: 13).
[43] Cushner (1976).
[44] Newson (2009).
[45] Cushner (1967) and Andaya (2009: 963–67).

dated 1734. Engraved by Nicolas de la Cruz Bagay and decorated by Francisco Suarez, both of whom were Filipinos, the map is strewn with galleon trading ships and Chinese junks. The cartouche enumerates the Islands' alleged natural resources including gold, pearls, cinnamon, indigo, medicinal herbs, and the New World plants, cacao, and tobacco. Around the map are vivid depictions of the cosmopolitan trading communities in the Islands, agricultural practices, and cultivation of useful plants including bamboo, betel, coconuts, and the New World fruits papaya and jackfruit (*nanca*). Clerics did not shy from hoarding earthly riches and had an eye for precious decorations, *alhajas*, and sacred vessels, *vasos sagrados*. They spent extravagantly. Religious purchases for San Agustin Church in the early seventeenth century included solid gold chalices from Mexico studded with diamonds, rubies, emeralds and amethysts, gold cruet sets, and reliquaries heavily embellished with precious jewels also from Mexico and gold bells from China.[46]

In the Visayas, commerce and trade occurred under the shadow of military defense. Since the fourteenth century, trade had been flourishing between Chinese merchants who passed via the Visayas to the Sulu Sea and Maluku, and the Visayan Ilonggos, who were skilled weavers and traded in cotton and sandalwood.[47] Agricultural production centered on rice cultivation and livestock-raising. Pan-ay island was agriculturally fertile and provided the main source of provisions and rice for the entire region, as well as Spanish expeditionary endeavors and military demands, supplying garrisons stationed in Mindanao and Ternate.[48] Spanish commercial activities began on Pan-ay, but Spaniards were initially compelled to address defense needs—establishing garrisons, forts, watchtowers, and their provisioning, in the Visayas, Maluku, and Mindanao that served against Muslim raiding and the Hispano-Dutch war (1621–1648). Missionization and militarization resulted in settlement and an increase in the population. As Linda Newson argues, depredations from Muslim raids in the early colonial period in the Visayas tended to encourage Christian conversion and settlement in missions, where Spanish priests organized better protection by establishing garrisons, providing weapons,

---

[46] Galende and Chua (2003: 5).
[47] McCoy (1982: 301).
[48] Newson (2009: 81).

and permitting use of the church as a site for defense. While the coastal town of Miag-ao reportedly suffered a raid in 1754, a garrison stationed along the southern coast was an effective deterrent from Moro raids.[49]

Protected from raids, benefiting from a burgeoning Christianized population, and prosperity from the textile trade, as discussed earlier in relation to Pan-ay's town church and the *piña* textile industry, Pan-ay's coastal towns—Tigbauan, San Joaquin, but most especially Miag-ao, possess some of the most spectacular church façades in the country, and considered to be the best examples of an indigenous variant of Mexican Churrigueresque style and strikingly vivid representations of New World flora and fauna. Regalado Trota José has speculated that in such towns, residents 'wholeheartedly' contributed labor and materials 'for what they perceived as an essentially spiritual service'. He conveys the impression of native collaboration in church building with whole families becoming involved in the process—men would cut and hew timber; women and children would ferry eggs and sand to the building site. In exchange for this work, José argues, the community was exempted from tribute, and recompensed in cash or in kind. For their efforts in helping to build San Joaquin's church, women received useful and much-needed articles such as steel sewing needles and thread.[50]

Papayas, Guavas, and Horses

Like the hill town churches of Laguna mentioned earlier, the Tigbauan Church, first built in 1787 and reconstructed during the second half of the nineteenth century, has a portal festooned with botanical carvings. The base of the pediment is decorated with floral motifs, as are the tapering pilasters; the spandrels are heavily ornamented with a wild tangle of interweaving vines and foliage. On the cornices are flat, cartwheel shaped flowers strung out in a chain which, scholars note, recall the delicate filigree design of the local *tambourin* necklace 'obviously', remarks Coseteng, 'an application of the goldsmith's art to architectural details'.[51]

---

[49] Newson (2009: 91–98).
[50] Trota José (1991: 30).
[51] Coseteng (1972: 98).

If the decoration of Tigbauan Church was largely confined to its portal, the churches at Miag-ao and its neighbor, San Joaquin, show far less restraint. Both made from the local ocher-colored carbonaceous limestone known as *tabriya* quarried from the mountains of Igbaras a few kilometers inland, these churches display an elaborate, luxuriousness of botanical detail and narrative drama. Built over a ten-year period, 1787–1797, in the Baroque-Romanesque style, the church in Miag-ao is situated at the highest point of the town. A single nave church, it is considered to be typical of a Spanish colonial mission church and follows the conventional Augustinian 'church-convento-atrium' configuration. Its walls are a meter and a half thick and reinforced with massive buttresses to resist earthquakes and typhoons. Bell towers on either side of the church are assumed to have served as observation posts. The left tower has four tiers topped by a low-pitched dome; the right tower is three-tiered and crowned by a steeply conical roof. Tower windows are narrow slit openings appear to give the towers 'Gothic and Romanesque aspects', while rounded and tapered corner buttresses are said to convey a 'robust medieval look'. These structural forms and features have led most observers to view Miag-ao church as a 'church-fortress', built to defend and repel raiders.[52]

Yet Miag-ao church is strikingly and uniquely decorated (Fig. 3). The façade features a stunning pediment decorated with a bas-relief sculpture of St. Christopher, native in garb and appearance, carrying the Christ Child and planting a fully grown coconut palm. Flanking him are luxuriant papaya and guava trees, the latter planted in vessels, perhaps stylized porcelain vases, their branches drooping under the weight of their luscious fruit (Fig. 4). Separated by the artifice of a balustrade, below the pediment is a stone image of St. Tomas de Villanueva, the town's patron saint and other statues and coats-of-arms that are difficult to identify. In charge of the work were two local *maestros-de-obras* of whom nothing is known.

Situated twelve kilometers from Miag-ao, the church at San Joaquin features a pediment whose surface decoration surpasses that of Miag-ao in terms of sophistication and detail (Fig. 5). Sources are in disagreement as to precisely when the church was built, and it is likely that the embellishments were later additions. The bas-relief commemorates the

---

[52] Rodríguez Rodríguez and Álvarez Fernández (undated: 471–84).

PARADISE IN STONE: REPRESENTATIONS OF NEW WORLD ... 63

Fig. 3 Miag-ao Church, pediment (Photo by Author)

Fig. 4 Miag-ao Church, pediment detail (Photo by Author)

Fig. 5 San Joaquin Church, pediment detail (Photo by Author)

Spanish victory against the Muslim Moroccan army in a battle fought at Tetuan, Morocco in 1860. Charged with action, movement, and energy, the scene compresses the activity of foot soldiers, horses, and their riders, who appear amidst lush flora and fauna—banana, coconut, and papaya trees, leaves, flowers, monkeys, and birds—that fill every available gap in the mural. It is a battle conducted in paradisiacal surroundings. The horses, notably, are beautifully formed—graceful, muscular, and powerful looking. Raising horses in Pan-ay had been done since at least the early seventeenth century, those in nearby Iloilo and its environs enjoyed the reputation of being the finest.[53]

Given the extravagant ornamentation, one might question whether Miag-ao church served real military needs. First, and most obviously, the elaborate sculptural decorations and the flanking bell towers do not seem appropriate or practical for the purpose of defense. Second, the Spaniards had established forts throughout the Island and there were forts in neighboring Iloilo and Otón. Further, an inventory of forts

[53] Newson (2009: 83).

from the Biblioteca Nacional de España in Madrid, dated 1739 commissioned by the Crown, details two other forts in Capiz and Romblon well supplied with firearms, powder, soldiers, and rice. Use of such an ornamented church for military needs perhaps seems rather wasteful. Third, a more instructive way of looking at highly elaborate church façades might be to see them as 'representations of conversion'. Scholars of Latin American architectural history, notably Elena Estrada de Gerlero, Jeanette Favrot Peterson, Santiago Sebastian have viewed the massive, aggressive-looking so-called fortress churches of New Spain, built with the aid of Christianized indigenous labor, as symbolizing spiritual fortresses, as an expression of a heavenly Jerusalem made manifest, insights that could well be applied to the Philippine context.[54]

DIDACTIC PURPOSES

In her careful examination of Mexico's sixteenth-century 'paradise garden murals' in the Augustinian monastic complex at Malinalco, Jeanette Favrot Peterson has argued that the lush garden scenes of flora and fauna painted in the murals can be understood as both an indigenous response and challenge to the utopian rhetoric of the Spanish Crown and regular clergy. The embellished pediments of the Miag-ao and San Joaquin churches are akin to the European graphic traditions found in New World colonial imagery and speak of a convergence between local realities and the utopian ideals of Catholicism and the State. The carved tableau of the Tetuan battle scene on the San Joaquin pediment, of course, not only commemorates the vanquishing of Spain's enemies but also confirms Spanish might. One can see the same visual strategy employed in images of St. James the Moorslayer, patron saint of Spain, which decorate the church in Paete mentioned earlier. However, in the Tetuan scene, a paradise surfaces through the interstices of battle and, arguably, also European utopian rhetoric and ideology, localizing and transforming a wholly unfamiliar historical event.

While these native features may have worked to advance the colonial mission of Church and State, is it also possible to see how they might have subverted it? The legend of St. Christopher bearing the Christ Child, the *Santo Niño*, whose cultural significance and popularity since

---

[54] Cited by Bargellini (1998: 94–95).

its arrival with Magellan shows no sign of abating, embodies the missionary task of bringing the Christian faith and planting it safely across from one shore to another. Instead of a staff to steady his stride, Christopher grasps the trunk of the coconut palm, widely revered throughout the archipelago for its life-giving uses. In the Malinalco murals, the ritually important *zapote* plant of the Aztecs was cast as the biblical Tree of Knowledge, a substitution that 'must have conveyed a non-Christian meaning and compromised the original Christian message' writes Peterson.[55] Use of the coconut palm, similarly, would surely be visually and emotionally appealing to the native viewer of Miag-ao, but one could not track with any certainty how the substitution might have undermined the orthodoxy of the message.

'FILIPINO' STYLE?

The wholesale adoption of the term 'Filipino' style has not just been a matter of semantics. The single word 'Filipino' was gradual replacement for the term 'Hispano-Filipino', to which Maria Lourdes Diaz-Trechuelo refers in her magisterial work *Arquitectura Espanola en Filipinas (1565–1800)* in 1959. Denoting a melding of culture and biology, 'Filipino' evoked blending and fusion. Pressed into service to define the nation's heterogeneous visual culture, the term, as Zialcita says, unified foreign cultural influences and the use of raw building materials native to the country's varied environments—timber from forests, stone from lava flows and reefs, shell from the seas, cane and leaves from grasses, all of which amounted to a blended style 'of different textures and traditions'.[56] Few have picked up on Alicia Coseteng's description of colonial churches as 'Oriental variant[s] of Caribbean and Latin American colonial architecture'.[57] The Hispanic inflection seems to have only just survived in the term *arquitectura mestiza* occasionally cited by scholars. Although the term brings to mind Angel Guido's use of the word *mestizo* in relation to the hybrid architecture of Latin America, Filipino scholars associate *arquitectura mestiza* with Ignacio Alcina, a seventeenth-century Jesuit residing in the Visayas for several decades,

---

[55] Peterson (1993: 9).
[56] Zialcita (1997: 11, cited in Invernizzi Tettoni 1997).
[57] Coseteng (1972: viii).

whose use of the term referred to the marriage of both stone and wood materials in constructing colonial buildings.[58]

Just as use of the term Filipino style has become commonplace, the application of labels such as 'Baroque' or 'Rococo' has been remarkably unproblematic. Few, it seems, have heeded Gauvin Alexander Bailey's caution that the terms, when applied in a global context, risk anachronism.[59] There is little qualification in claims of widespread 'baroquization of Philippine religious architecture' of the eighteenth and early nineteenth centuries,[60] or that the rococo label could only be appropriately used to describe a decorative style,[61] or that local baroque adaptations possessing American or Muslim characteristics suggest indigenous expressiveness. Thus, a host of early modern churches throughout Luzon and the Visayas richly ornamented, featuring flat, symmetrical, planimetric art, displaying an innovative and complex artistic convergence and syncretism, utterly devoid of stylistic unity, is shown to manifest Filipino visual culture: The portal of the Tigbauan Church in Iloilo on the island of Pan-ay in the Visayas, for instance, draws upon 'Churrigueresque' style, while Daraga church in Albay, Bikol, in Morong, Rizal, Paete in Laguna, and the Miag-ao church in Pan-ay revel in rococo fantasies.[62]

Central to the 'Filipino style' interpretation is indigenous agency and its visibility, and the key assumption that indigenous elements may be recognized, teased apart and described. In the Philippine case, the involvement of indigenous labor is speculative in most examples. Legarda is inclined to give initial credit to Chinese artisans for the execution of decorative stonework, who then transferred their knowledge and technology to Filipinos.[63] The fact is, where they have surfaced in the archival records, largely at the beginning of the eighteenth century, the data on indigenous artisans remains slim, restricted in general to the names of master builders, masons, and carpenters that occasionally crop up and that are, at best, suggestive of ethnicity and conversion to Christianity. Another sticking point is that even where native sculptors can be

---

[58] Trota José (1991: 32) and Trota José (2003: 13).
[59] Bailey (1999: 26).
[60] Coseteng (1972: 4).
[61] Trota José (1984).
[62] Coseteng (1972: 5).
[63] Legarda Personal Email Communication to the Author, dated June 25, 2018.

identified, is it also not possible to say with any degree of certainty that they were able to determine what could be represented.

A more insurmountable problem lies in the fact that there is little in the way of extant pre-colonial figurative art and a complete absence of pre-colonial stone temple structures from which direct references and local comparisons might be made. Scholars instead have turned to native artistic traditions for evidence. As we have seen, wood carving is frequently cited in support of the oft-made claim that Filipinos love to embellish, but this in itself makes for a flimsy explanation for ornate surface decoration on stone churches. Weaving or, to take another example, gold working, in the Philippines, is several millennia old, dating back to at least the tenth century in the case of gold working. The designs, patterns, and motifs appearing on these materials are complex, intricately rendered, decorative, and delicate. A close examination of gold work reveals a marked familiarity with Hindu-Buddhist concepts and Chinese mythology suggesting processes of transcultural transmission.[64] Stone carvings of flora and fauna are far from unknown and have a visual heritage in island Southeast Asia of great antiquity. In neighboring Java, in the Indonesian archipelago, the narrative bas-reliefs on the monumental ninth-century-Buddhist stupa of Borobudur exult in visual representations of plants and animals both local and foreign.[65] The strength of the evidence depends principally on drawing on a large number of comparisons from several cultures and figuring in complex factors related to anthropology and archaeology. However, to date there have been no serious attempts to demonstrate a stylistic dialogue and draw resemblances and connections between these ancient artistic practices and the embellishments on eighteenth-century churches.

In reckoning with the mixed, hybrid nature of colonial church decoration, nationalist perspectives have sought to isolate specifically indigenous modes of sculpting and building. Writing on hybridity and visual culture in colonial Spanish America, Carolyn Dean, and Dana Leibsohn recently argued that choosing or not choosing to recognize and name hybridity are acts that owe something to present needs and desires, bound up with efforts 'to see and know what is disquieting about

---

[64] Capistrano-Baker (2011: 75).
[65] Cammerloher (1923), Steinmann (1934, 1961), and Miksic (1990).

colonial history'. In this regard, what is made visible or invisible are highly problematic maneuvers, entangled in conventions of seeing.[66]

Might we then see the putative Filipino style, deemed to be distinctively local, if not native, in origin, design, composition, as a notion freighted with nationalist investments? Interpretations of Filipino style and its recognition, it seems, ultimately derives power from where Filipino style appears: upon colonial structures that have the distinction of being known as quintessential symbols of Spanish imperial might, conquest, and domination.[67]

The exuberant floral and faunal surface decorations that embellish the Baroque Hispanic churches of the Philippines have come to be considered by Philippine architectural historians as native expressions—manifesting local originality and reflective of a 'love of the ornate'. Alicia Coseteng has argued that these decorative elements 'show a peculiar affinity…to the *tequitqui*' artistic style of religious sculptures found in sixteenth-century Mexican churches, in which indigenous forms hybridize Euro-Christian visual and architectural traditions. Unlike Latin America, building in stone has no historical antecedent in the Philippines and without more pre-colonial artistic evidence for comparison, identifying what is indigenous with clarity and distinction is problematic. The use of floral and faunal motifs and paradisical imagery, the prominent role given to New World plants in the Philippine Hispanic context, provoke many difficult questions regarding symbolism, adaptation and subversion, and the social conditions of their production.

One further issue, which this chapter did not fully explore, is the control of space. The erection of monumental buildings and their significant occupation of space served the agenda of the friars, but in what ways did they serve the indigenous population who collaborated in their construction?

If it is possible to find clear native modifications and some pattern to those modifications, then perhaps Filipino style may come to be defined not in the indigenous sense necessarily, but as complex acts of mediation between Catholicism and European church personnel, local artisans and their efforts, and the social, cultural, material, and historical conditions that emerged within the Philippine setting.

---

[66] Dean and Leibsohn (2003).
[67] See in particular Constantino (1975).

Acknowledgements I incurred many debts in the research and writing of this chapter. I especially thank Professor Thomas DaCosta Kaufmann at Princeton University, who urged me to look more closely at Philippine churches, and for his insightful comments and many references. I benefited much from Professor Benito Legarda's intimate knowledge of church architecture in northern Philippines. He generously read my draft chapters and sent extensive comments that were genial and inspiring. Much thanks are also due to David Alvarez Cineira, archivist at the Augustinian seminary, Valladolid, Spain; Arsenio Rafael who welcomed me in Iloilo; and Jim Richardson for his sound advice. Research took me all over the Philippines, looking and photographing churches. I thank members of my family, especially Gaia Tera Vida Reyes, who accompanied me over several summers since 2010.

BIBLIOGRAPHY

Alvina, Corazon S., and Domingo A. Madulid. 2009. *Flora Filipina: From Acapulco to Manila*. Manila: Art Post Asia and National Museum of the Philippines.

Andaya, Barbara. 2009. Between Empires and Emporia: The Economics of Christianization in Early Modern Southeast Asia. In Jos Gommans (ed.). Empires and Emporia: The Orient and World Historical Space and Time. *Journal of the Economic and Social History of the Orient* 52 (4–5): 963–967.

A Primera Viagem Histórica da Globalização in *Revista de Cultura* International Edition 17, January 2006 (Instituto Cultural de Macao).

Bailey, Gauvin Alexander. 1999. *Art on the Jesuit Missions in Asia and Latin America, 1542–1773*. Toronto: University of Toronto Press.

Bankoff, Greg. 2004. Horsing Around: The Life and Times of the Horse in the Philippines at the Turn of the Twentieth Century. In *Smallholders and Stockbreeders: Histories of Foodcrop and Livestock Farming in Southeast Asia*, ed. Peter Boomgaard and David Henley. Leiden: KITLV Press.

Bargellini, Clara. 1998. Representations of Conversion: Sixteenth-Century Architecture in New Spain. In *The Word Made Image: Religion, Art, and Architecture in Spain and Spanish America, 1500–1600*. Boston: Trustees of the Isabella Stewart Gardner Museum.

Bernal, Rafael. 1965. *Mèxico en Filipinas: estudio de una transculturación*. Mexico: Universidad Nacional Autónoma de Mèxico.

Boomgaard, Peter. 1999. Maize and Tobacco in Upland Indonesia, 1600–1940. In *Transforming the Indonesian Uplands*, ed. Tania Murray Li, 45–79. Amsterdam: Harwood Academic Publishers.

Boomgaard, Peter. 2003a. The High Sanctuary: Local Perceptions of Mountains in Indonesia, 1750–2000. In *Framing Indonesian Realities: Essays in Symbolic Anthropology in Honour of Reimar Schefold*, ed. Peter Nas, Gerard Persoon, and Rivke Jaffe, 295–315. Leiden: KITLV Press.

Boomgaard, Peter. 2003b. In the Shadow of Rice: Roots and Tubers in Indonesian History, 1500–1950. *Agricultural History* 77 (4): 582–610.
Boomgaard, Peter, and Marjolein 't Hart (eds.). 2010. Globalization, Environmental Change and Social History. *International Instituut voor Geschiedenis* 55 (Suppl.): 1–26.
Cammerloher, H. 1923. Die Pflanzendarstellungen auf den Reliefs des Borobudur (Mitteljava). *Natur illustrierte Halbmonatschrift für Naturfreunde* 14: 222–229.
Capistrano-Baker, Florina. 2011. *Philippine Ancestral Gold.* Makati: Ayala Museum and NUS Press.
Christie, Jan Wisseman. 1992. Water from the Ancestors: Irrigation in Early Java and Bali. In *The Gift of Water: Water Management, Cosmology and the State in Southeast Asia*, ed. Jonathan Rigg, 7–25. London: SOAS.
Constantino, Renato. 1975. *The Philippines: A Past Revisted.* London and New York: Monthly Review Press.
Coseteng, Alice. 1972. *Spanish Churches in the Philippines.* Quezon City: UNESCO National Commission of the Philippines.
Crosby, Alfred. 1972. *The Columbian Exchange: Biological and Cultural Consequences of 1492.* Westport, CT: Greenwood.
Cushner, Nicholas P. 1967. Merchants and Missionaries: A Theologian's View of Clerical Involvement in the Galleon Trade. *The Hispanic American Historical Review* 47: 360–369.
Cushner, Nicholas P. 1971. *Spain in the Philippines: From Conquest to Revolution.* Quezon City: Charles E. Tuttle.
Cushner, Nicholas P. 1976. Landed Estates in the Colonial Philippines. Monograph Series No. 20, Yale University Southeast Asia Studies, New Haven.
David-Perez, Enriqueta. 1973. *Recipes of the Philippines.* Mandaluyong: Cacho Hermanos.
Dean, Carolyn, and Dana Leibsohn. 2003. Hybridity and Its Discontents: Considering Visual Culture in Colonial Spanish America. *Colonial Latin American Review* 12 (1): 27–35.
De Jesus, Ed. C. 1998. *The Tobacco Monopoly: Bureaucratic Enterprise and Social Change 1766–1880.* Manila: Ateneo de Manila University Press.
De la Costa, H., S.J. 1961. *The Jesuits in the Philippines, 1581–1768.* Cambridge, Mass: Harvard University Press.
Endangered Fil-Hispanic Architecture: Papers from the First International Congress on Fil-Hispanic Architecture. 2005. Manila: Instituto Cervantes de Manila.
Fernandez, Doreen D., and Edilberto N. Alegre. 1988. *Sarap: Essays on Philippine Food.* Manila: Mr. and Ms. Publishing Co.
Flores, Patrick D. 1998. *Painting History: Revisions in Philippine Colonial Art.* Quezon City: University of the Philippines Press.

Flynn, Dennis O., Lionel Frost, and A.J.H. Latham (eds.). 1999. *Pacific Centuries: Pacific and Pacific Rim History Since the Sixteenth Century*. London and New York: Routledge.

Flynn, Dennis O., Arturo Giráldez, and James Sobredo (eds.). 2001. European Entry into the Pacific: Spain and the Acapulco-Manila Galleons. In *The Pacific World: Lands, Peoples and History of the Pacific, 1500–1900 Series*, vol. 4. Aldershot: Ashgate.

Galende, Pedro O.S.A. 1987. *Angels in Stone: Architecture of Augustinian Churches in the Philippines*. Manila: G. F. Formoso.

Galende, Pedro G., and Clifford T. Chua. 2003. *The Gold and Silver Collection: San Agustin Museum, Intramuros, Manila*. Manila: National Commission for Culture and the Arts.

Galván, Javier. 2001. Arquitectura Fil-Hispánica en el valle del río Cagayán. In *Imperios y Naciones en el Pacífico*, vol. II, ed. Ma. Dolores Elizalde, Josep M. Fradera, and Luis Alonso, 292–311. Madrid: Consejo Superior de Investigaciones Cientificas.

Giraldez, Arturo. 2015. *The Age of Trade: The Manila Galleons and the Dawn of the Global Economy*. London: Rowman & Littlefield.

Guillermo, Alice. 2001. *Image to Meaning: Essays on Philippine Art*. Quezon City: Ateneo de Manila University Press.

Guzman-Rivas, Pablo. 1960. Reciprocal Geographic Influences of the Trans-Pacific Galleon Trade. Unpublished PhD dissertation, University of Texas, Austin.

Harris, Hugh. 2012. Key to Coconut Cultivation on the American Pacific Coast: The Manila–Acapulco Galleon Route (1565–1815). *Palms* 56 (2): 72–77.

Hila, Corazon. 1992. *Arkitektura: An Essay on Philippine Ethnic Architecture*. Manila: Sentrong Pangkultura ng Pilipinas.

Impelluso, Lucia. 2004. *Nature and Its Symbols: A Guide to Imagery*. Los Angeles: The J. Paul Getty Museum.

Invernizzi Tettoni, Luca. 1997. *Filipino Style*. London: Thames and Hudson.

Javellana, Rene B. 1991. S.J. *Wood and Stone for God's Greater Glory: Jesuit Art and Architecture in the Philippines*. Manila: Ateneo de Manila University Press.

Javellana, Rene B. 1997. S.J. *Fortress of Empire: Spanish Colonial Fortifications of the Philippines*. Manila: Bookmark Inc.

Javellana, Rene B. 2010. S.J. *La Casa de Dios: The Legacy of Filipino-Hispanic Churches in the Philippines*. Metro Manila: Ortigas Foundation.

Kelemen, Pal. 1951. *Baroque and Rococo in Latin America*. New York: Macmillan.

Legarda, Benito J. Jr. 1960. Colonial Churches of Ilocos. *Philippine Studies* 8 (1): 121–158.

Legarda, Benito J. Jr. 1981. Angels in Clay: The Typical Cagayan Church Style. In *The Filipinas Journal of Science and Culture*, vol. II, 69–81. Manila: Filipinas Foundation Inc.
Legarda, Benito J. Jr. 1999. *After the Galleons: Foreign Trade, Economic Change and Entrepreneurship in the Nineteenth-Century Philippines*. Quezon City: Ateneo de Manila University Press.
Lubinsky, Pesach, Kenneth M. Cameron, María Carmen Molina, Maurice Wong, Sandra Lepers-Andrzejewski, Arturo Gómez-Pompa, and Seung-Chul Kim. 2008. Neotropical Roots of a Polynesian Spice: The Hybrid Origin of Tahitian Vanilla, *Vanilla Tahitensis* (ORCHIDACEAE). *American Journal of Botany* 95 (8): 1040–1047.
McCoy, Alfred W. 1982. A Queen Dies Slowly: The Rise and Decline of Iloilo City. In *Philippine Social History: Global Trade and Local Transformations*, ed. Alfred W. McCoy and Ed. C. De Jesus. Sydney: Asian Studies Association of Australia and George Allen and Unwin.
Miksic, John. 1990. *Borobudur: Golden Tales of the Buddhas*. Hong Kong: Periplus Editions.
Milgram, B. Lyn. 2009. Piña Cloth, Identity and the Project of Nationalism. *Asian Studies Review* 29: 233–246.
Montinola, Lourdes R. 1991. *Piña*. Manila: Amon Foundation.
Newson, Linda A. 2009. *Conquest and Pestilence in the Early Spanish Philippines*. Manoa: University of Hawaii Press.
Of War and Peace: Lantakas and Bells in Search for Foundries in the Philippines. 2009. Manila: UST Publishing House.
Perez, Rodrigo D. 1989. *Arkitektura: An Essay on Philippine Architecture*. Manila: Sentrong Pangkultura ng Pilipinas.
Peterson, Jeanette Favrot. 1993. *The Paradise Garden Murals of Malinalco: Utopia and Empire in Sixteenth-Century Mexico*. Austin: University of Texas Press.
Reyes, Raquel A.G. 2017. Flaunting It: How the Galleon Trade Made Manila, Circa. 1571–1800. *Early American Studies* 15 (4) (Fall): 683–714.
Rodríguez Rodríguez, Isacio, and Jesús Álvarez Fernández. n.d. *Miagao: arte y fe en diálogo amistoso*, 471–84.
Seijas, Tatiana. 2014. *Asian Slaves in Colonial Mexico: From Chinos to Indians*. New York, NY: Cambridge University Press.
Smith, Stefan Halikowski. 2015. In the Shadow of a Pepper-Centric Historiography: Understanding the Global Diffusion of Capsicums in the Sixteenth and Seventeenth Centuries. *Journal of Ethnopharmacology* 167: 73–74.
Smith, Winfield Scott III (ed.). 1958. *The Art of the Philippines, 1521–1957*, 1–10. Manila: Associated Publishers.

Spate, O.H.K. 1979. *The Spanish Lake*. London: Croom Helm.
Spinola, Maria Lourdes Diaz-Trechuelo. 1959. *Arquitectura española en Filipinas, 1565–1800*. Sevilla: Escuela de Estudios Hispano-Americanos de Sevilla.
Steinmann, A. 1934. De op de Boroboedoer afgebeelde Plantenwereld. *Bijdrage Tot de Geschied* 74: 581–612.
Steinmann, A. 1961. De Afbeeldingen van planten op de spuiers van Djalatoenda. *BKI* 117: 357–361.
Tremml-Werner, Birgit. 2015. *Spain, China and Japan in Manila, 1571–1644: Local Comparisons, Global Connections*. Amsterdam: Amsterdam University Press.
Trota José, Regalado. 1984. How to Recognize Rococo Art. *Art Collector* (September–October), 16–32.
Trota José, Regalado. 1990. *Images of Faith: Religious Ivory Carvings from the Philippines*. Pasadena: Pacific Asia Museum.
Trota José, Regalado. 1991. *Simbahan: Church Art in Colonial Philippines, 1565–1898*. Manila: Ayala Museum.
Trota José, Regalado. 2002. Lumang Simbahan: Ancestral Churches of Batangas. In *Batangas: Forged in Fire*, ed. Ramon N. Villegas. Makati City: Ayala Foundation.
Trota José, Regalado. 2003. *Zero In: Skin, Surface, Essence*. Manila: Ateneo Art Gallery.
Zialcita, Fernando Nakpil. 2005. *Authentic Though Not Exotic: Essays on Filipino Identity*. Quezon City: Ateneo de Manila University Press.

Betel, Tobacco and Beverages in Southeast Asia

William Gervase Clarence-Smith

Abstract There remains a historical puzzle concerning the sudden collapse in the popularity of betel chewing in Southeast Asia. A custom that was addictive, and that had become deeply entrenched in local culture over millennia, all but vanished with remarkable speed. This chapter focuses on the changing social and cultural attitudes that can lead to sudden alterations in tastes. It explores the intimately intertwined roles of religion, tobacco and hot beverages, namely tea, coffee and chocolate (cocoa), from around the sixteenth century. While cigarettes were beneficiaries of the decline of betel, this was true mainly of masculine consumption. For women, hot beverages were better placed than tobacco to substitute for betel. With such beverages popularized by world religions, secular reformers were in a better position to launch campaigns against betel.

Keywords South East Asia · Stimulants · Betel · Tobacco · Tea · Coffee · Chocolate

W. G. Clarence-Smith (✉)
School of Oriental and African Studies (SOAS),
University of London, London, UK

Introduction[1]

Physical properties and psychology may account for the choice of relaxing or stimulating products that are not central to nutrition, as may symbolic functions associated with religious rituals and social practices.[2] Various plants produce bitter alkaloids, as insecticides or herbicides. When ingested by human beings, alkaloids alter perceptions and mental functions to varying degrees.[3] Nicotine is the chief mind-altering substance contained in tobacco, arecoline in the areca nut of the betel quid, caffeine in tea and coffee and theobromine in chocolate.[4] People may cling tenaciously to an accustomed product, or may switch to a new one.[5] Whether alkaloids are physically or psychologically addictive, or both, remains a hotly debated topic, even in the case of opiates.[6] Opium, cannabis and alcoholic beverages are only intermittently considered in this chapter, although they too were rivals in consumption practices.[7]

In a widely cited and influential article, Anthony Reid argues that smoking tobacco displaced the venerable and ancient Indonesian practice of chewing betel (*sirih*).[8] This argument has been extended to Southeast Asia as a whole.[9] However, Reid skates over the gender issue unconvincingly and distorts the part played by religion. Moreover, he fails to note that other new competitors to betel began to spread at about the same time as tobacco, from around the sixteenth century, namely tea, coffee and chocolate (cocoa).[10]

---

[1] Originally presented as a paper at the Workshop 'Plants, people, consumption and work: the social history of cash crops in Asia, 18th to 20th centuries,' Gadjah Mada University and International Institute of Social History, Yogyakarta, 13–15 August 2009. My thanks are due to the organizers.

[2] Goodman et al. (1995), Schivelbusch (1992), and Matthee (2005).

[3] Hesse (2002: Ch. 9).

[4] Goodman (1993), Jana (2006), Barr (1998), and Coe and Michael (1996).

[5] Goodman et al. (1995) and Schivelbusch (1992).

[6] Dikötter et al. (2004).

[7] Reid (1985: 540), for opium.

[8] Reid (1985).

[9] Rooney (1993: 66–67) and Reichart and Philipsen (1996: 66).

[10] Clarence-Smith (2008).

THE RISE OF BETEL IN SOUTHEAST ASIA

Chewing is one of the most ancient and widespread human habits, and the betel quid is among the oldest of human chews, if not the oldest. The consumer wraps a betel leaf (*Piper betle*) around sliced areca nuts (*Areca catechu*) and adds slaked lime to extract alkaloids more effectively. A host of other products makes the quid more aromatic, astringent or stimulating. Areca 'nuts' are the fruit of a tall and graceful palm, and their intoxicating effects are greatest when they are green and fresh, but they are also consumed dried or smoked. As for betel leaves, harvested from a vine related to the pepper vine, they contain an essential oil similar to that of cloves. The leaves offset the astringency of the areca nuts, sweeten the breath and disinfect the mouth. Both the areca palm and the betel vine grow best in low-lying, hot and humid environments, close to the sea. The betel vine may be grown on the areca palm. Whereas areca nuts are readily exported in a preserved state, the betel leaf should be consumed fresh, or at least blanched, and is difficult to trade over any distance.[11]

The first indications of betel in Southeast Asia come from finds of areca nuts in a Thai cave, dating from around 10,000 BCE, and thus predating systematic agriculture. Further discoveries in Thailand have been made from between 7000 and 3000 BCE. Moreover, skeletons from around 3000 BCE in the Philippines suggest that the areca nut was chewed. Together with evidence for wild varieties of areca and betel, this suggests that the betel quid originated in Southeast Asia. It later spread across the Indian Ocean to India and East Africa, up the South China littoral and across the western half of the South Pacific.[12]

Epigraphic and linguistic data on betel, as well as chronicles and legends, are common for the period before the arrival of the Portuguese.[13] Early modern observers reported on the omnipresence of betel chewing.[14] It was even asserted that local people would prefer to give up food

---

[11] Penzer (1952), Thierry (1969), Rooney (1993), Reichart and Philipsen (1996), and Jana (2006).

[12] Rooney (1993: 5–14) and Reichart and Philipsen (1996: 12). See also Penzer (1952).

[13] Matsuyama (2003: 106, 111, 139), Reid (1988: 42–44), Thierry (1969: 15, 191–92), Rooney (1993: 15), Gode (1961: 128–29, 166–67), Penzer (1952: 211), Reichart and Philipsen (1996: 39), and Bigalke (2005: 112).

[14] Loureiro (2007), Matsuyama (2003: 232), Reid (1988: 42–45), Rooney (1993: 8), Sangermano (1966: 157–58), Nguyen (1965: 87), Li and Reid (1993: 77–78), Galvão (1971: 43, 57, 115), and Gode (1961: 123–26).

rather than betel, and that they would die if deprived of their favourite quid.[15] Consumption penetrated to the lowest classes, with the Dutch calling the small sums occasionally given to slaves 'betel money.'[16] French clerics noted that seventeenth-century Ayudhya taxes on areca and betel were set at a low rate, and yet brought in considerable sums for the treasury.[17]

Abundant evidence from the nineteenth century shows that high levels of betel chewing continued to prevail in Southeast Asia.[18] Prince Dipanagara, leader of the Java War of 1825–1830, chewed betel constantly and 'even reckoned the passage of time by how long it took to masticate mouthfuls.'[19] Smallholders grew areca palms everywhere around their villages, and veritable commercial plantations emerged in places such as southern Thailand.[20] Thai exports of areca nuts to India, China and Malaya were significant, while Sumatra sent them to Penang for redistribution.[21]

Ritually associated with central moments in the life cycle, betel was especially significant in customs surrounding marriage and love, and in establishing contact with the spirit world after death. Betel thus gave rise to an artistically decorated and highly elaborated paraphernalia of objects, used to contain and carry ingredients, cut areca nuts and receive saliva. Indeed, betel sets are reckoned to be among the finest and earliest examples of the decorative arts in Southeast Asia.[22]

That said, other masticatories were also present in parts of Southeast Asia, notably tea in its initial forms. A source of caffeine, tea was chewed and eaten in the tangled mountains where Southeast Asia meets India and China, where *Camellia sinensis* has its botanical origins.[23] Leaves were picked from wild trees. Fermented or pickled, they were rolled into

[15] Rooney (1993: 1) and Reid (1985: 530).
[16] Reid (1985: 542).
[17] Thierry (1969: 192).
[18] Low (1972: 69), Neale (1852: 153–55), Young (1900: 90–99), Penzer (1952: 256–58, 260–61, 264–65), Rooney (1993: 1, 5, 8–10), and Mertel (2002: 5).
[19] Carey (2007: 122, and also 697, 718).
[20] Reichart and Philipsen (1996: 53), Rooney (1993: 3), and Penzer (1952: 256–57).
[21] Low (1972: 72), Rooney (1993: 24), and Penzer (1952: 256).
[22] Penzer (1952), Thierry (1969), Rooney (1993), and Reichart and Philipsen (1996).
[23] Lieberman (2003: 175), Gardella (1994: 22–23), and Macfarlane and Macfarlane (2003: 42–43).

wads for chewing and were also sometimes eaten with salt, as a kind of vegetable. Known as *miang* in northern Thailand, such forms of tea were first noted around 1500. Lacking a well-developed associated set of rituals and objects, the consumption of *miang* probably developed later than that of betel.[24] Fermented tea was common in Burma earlier, from at least the thirteenth century, and was often chewed in parallel with betel.[25] Tea cultivation grew slowly, probably spilling over into highland Burma from southern Yunnan from around 1500.[26]

The Decline of Betel in Southeast Asia

Modern ideas, spread by education, rather suddenly undermined the consumption of betel.[27] From the late nineteenth century, with the triumph of germ theory, spitting was accused of spreading disease, especially tuberculosis. Chewing was associated with oral cancer from the 1930s. Medical personnel decried the addictiveness of areca nuts, and dentists criticized their effects on teeth and gums. Social and aesthetic critics rejected the emission of copious blood-red saliva and the blackening of teeth.[28] While black and filed teeth had distinguished humans from animals, white and whole teeth were now prized.[29]

The retrogression of betel chewing in Southeast Asia varied in time and was socially uneven. European men in West Java generally stopped chewing as early as the mid-eighteenth century, although their wives, often locally born, kept up the habit into the early nineteenth century.[30] The latter period coincided with efforts by Dutch and British reformers to Westernize elite culture in Java, with European officials ceasing to offer betel to Javanese guests after 1808.[31] The Javanese elite had mostly

---

[24] Reichart and Philipsen (1996: 123–24, 129).
[25] Lieberman (2003: 175, 178, 196–97), Sangermano (1966: 86–87, 175–77, 217–18), and Symes (1995: 273, 365, 412).
[26] Lieberman (2003: 175) and Butel (1989: 132).
[27] Rooney (1993: 66–67).
[28] Reid (1985: 538), Gupta and Ray (2004), Parsell (2005), Reichart and Philipsen (1996: 37), Rooney (1993: 6–7, 26–29, 67), Penzer (1952: 290–98), and Mertel (2002: 17).
[29] Penzer (1952: 292–93).
[30] Reid (1985: 538).
[31] Carey (2007: 166).

abandoned betel by the onset of the twentieth century, although their 'betel set was ritually carried around on all formal occasions.' Educated Indonesians viewed the quid as unprogressive, unhygienic and uncivilized, as well as a stumbling block to finding employment. In West Sumatra, known for its high levels of education, young men were at the forefront of abandoning betel in 1905, as part of an adoption of Western manners, chewing only 'when courting... or during feasts and rituals.' In South Sulawesi, it was said that almost everybody chewed in 1900, but that almost nobody did so in 1950, even if betel sets were still passed on as family heirlooms and served in marriage rituals.[32]

Reid's description is Java-centric, and somewhat exaggerates the speed and thoroughness of betel's decline in Indonesia, even in Java itself. Ponder's vignettes of Java in the 1930s indicate how widespread betel remained, 'the "chew" without which no Javanese would find life endurable.'[33] Collet considered betel chewing to be universal in Sumatra in 1925.[34] In the eastern Lesser Sunda Islands of Indonesia, betel continues to this day to form a significant part of the expenditure of ordinary people, especially in rural areas.[35]

There are similar problems with dating change in the Malayan peninsula. Frank Swettenham asserted in 1907: 'Now the chewing of betel has gone so completely out of fashion that it is seldom seen.'[36] Two years later, R. O. Winstedt noted more cautiously that the 'younger generation' had turned against the red saliva and black teeth caused by betel.[37] But colonial officials referred to the urban middle class, not the masses.[38] A study of domestic consumption in Malaysia from 1940 to 1964 revealed that, apart from rice, betel remained 'the most important item for daily use of a family living in rural areas.'[39] Indeed, some betel chewing persists among Malays to our own times.[40]

---

[32] Reid (1985: 531, 536, 538–39).
[33] Ponder (1990: 180). See also pp. 48, 53, 71–72, 131, 181–82.
[34] Penzer (1952: 265–66).
[35] Roger Montgomery, personal communication.
[36] Swettenham (1907: 149).
[37] Penzer (1952: 261).
[38] Macmillan (1925: 442).
[39] Rooney (1993: 66).
[40] Gupta and Ray (2004: 32).

In the Philippines, a similar urban bias overstates the speed and extent of the retreat of betel. In towns, Western ideas of hygiene and progress have greatly reduced chewing. In Manila, betel is now seen as a reprehensible addiction of South Asian immigrants. In the countryside, however, most markets stock abundant supplies of areca nut, fresh betel leaf and prepared lime.[41]

In independent Thailand, there was no sign of any crisis in betel consumption prior to the military coup of 1932.[42] Indeed, in 1882–1883, there were 7,644,915 areca palms registered for taxation purposes, with plantations concentrated in the south of the country.[43] A few years later, it was reported that 'great cargoes [of areca nuts] are shipped to India and China.' Moreover, foreign visitors lambasted 'this abominable habit of betel nut chewing,' which remained very widespread.[44]

After 1932, however the new Thai regime subjected its population to a degree of official repression that went far beyond what any colonial authorities would have dared to consider. In particular, the authoritarian Field-Marshal Phibunsongkhram sought to achieve rapid modernization and Westernization from 1938.[45] Nationalist arguments for the restriction of betel chewing became ever more strident. In terms of the 1942 Act of National Culture, Thais were ordered to cease spitting betel-stained saliva in public places.[46] In 1945, a new law banned the chewing of betel altogether, as it was an 'un-European and uncivilized' custom.[47] Although this law was hard to enforce, officials proceeded to oversee the chopping down of thousands of hectares of areca palms.[48]

As the Thai regime gradually became more liberal after World War II, people resumed chewing betel openly, but the custom did not recover its former prominence. In northern Thai villages in the early 1950s, it was those over the age of 35 who chewed, whereas 'the younger villagers today very definitely have been indoctrinated in school against betel

---

[41] Mertel (2002: 6, 17).
[42] Penzer (1952: 256–57).
[43] Reichart and Philipsen (1996: 53).
[44] Rooney (1993: 3, 5, 10, 24).
[45] Wyatt (1982: 254–55).
[46] Reichart and Philipsen (1996: 61, 65).
[47] Rooney (1993: 66).
[48] Baas Terwiel, personal communication.

chewing...'[49] In Bangkok itself, the habit declined fast. The harvest of southern areca plantations was increasingly exported, together with 'fermented' betel leaf from orchards in the south.[50] Chewing betel was increasingly confined to poor, old, rural women. The young sported gleaming white teeth and chewed American gum.[51]

Indochina reveals a mixed picture. In Cambodia and southern Vietnam, farmers still raised areca palms and betel vines quite intensively as late as the 1960s, although Cambodia's traditional exports of areca nuts to southern and central Vietnam ceased after 1945.[52] Following the launching of Vietnam's recent reform process, there have been signs of a slight resurgence of betel chewing among young Vietnamese, and the estimated 5% of Vietnamese who chew seems slightly higher than in neighbouring countries. There may be cultural influence from Taiwan, where the betel habit has witnessed a remarkable resurgence of late.[53]

Despite caveats about the timing and extent of decline, it is broadly true that a custom culturally engrained for millennia in Southeast Asia largely vanished within a matter of half a century or so. Moreover, the decline of betel sprang from ideas about modernity, civility and hygiene. The main controversy thus concerns what replaced betel, and it is here that Reid's hypothesis is weakest.

THE RISE OF TOBACCO

After the Iberians brought tobacco from the Americas in the late sixteenth century, its use and cultivation spread quickly.[54] The Spaniards introduced the crop into the Philippines in 1575, and both the plant and smoking may have diffused from there.[55] Tobacco became the 'bread and wine' of the local population. Cigars were the common form of consumption, with chopped shreds placed in a wrapper leaf of tobacco, but powdered snuff was also inhaled.[56] By 1782, the tobacco habit was so

---

[49] Reichart and Philipsen (1996: 65).
[50] Thierry (1969: 191) and Reichart and Philipsen (1996: 61–62).
[51] Reichart and Philipsen (1996: 52, 65–66, 129).
[52] Thierry (1969: 229–30, 255).
[53] Nguyen and Reichart (2008).
[54] de Jonge (1988: 91).
[55] Reid (1985: 535–36).
[56] de Jesus (1982: 28) and Mallat (1983: 89–90).

ingrained in the islands that the Spanish crown created a state monopoly, on lines pioneered in the Americas, which lasted for a century. The Spaniards thereby placed their finances in the islands on a sound footing for the first time and even remitted funds to the metropolis for a few decades.[57]

The spread of tobacco to Mainland Southeast Asia is not well documented, but it was present in Vietnam in 1622, albeit used less than betel.[58] In the mid-eighteenth century, Vietnamese men carried both betel and tobacco pouches.[59] 'Cheroots,' probably meaning hand-rolled cigarettes, were also being smoked in Burma and Thailand by the end of the seventeenth century.[60]

The Kartasura chronicle dates 'the first tobacco' and 'the beginning of the people smoking' in central Java with surprising precision, at the death of a ruler in 1601–1602.[61] Java's court was a focus for the growing social acceptance of tobacco, albeit in tandem with betel. The pipe was the implement of the elite, but there also grew up a custom of hand-rolling shredded tobacco in leaves of maize, bananas or palms, with spices sometimes added.[62] Tobacco allegedly became second only to rice on Java, as a crop cultivated for the internal market.[63]

However, there followed a marked decline of smoking in Java and beyond, probably from around the 1750s. John Crawfurd even asserted that smoking was 'generally discontinued,' at the time of the British occupation of the island in 1811–1816.[64] However, Prince Dipanagara indulged in hand-rolled cigarettes and cigarillos, as well as betel and a little wine.[65] Nevertheless, Low considered that Malays smoked little in the 1830s, compared to Chinese with their pipes.[66]

The novelty was that the Javanese increasingly took shredded tobacco leaf orally, in association with betel. European sailors generally chewed

---

[57] de Jesus (1980).
[58] Dror and Taylor (2006: 102).
[59] Li and Reid (1993: 78).
[60] Reid (1992: 498).
[61] Reid (1985: 535).
[62] Reid (1985: 535–36), Castles (1967: 32–33), and de Jonge (1988: 92).
[63] de Jonge (1988: 91).
[64] Reid (1985: 537–38).
[65] Carey (2007: 122–23).
[66] Low (1972: 67).

tobacco, as smoking was a mortal peril in wooden ships, whereas the Javanese placed a wad of it between lip and gum after chewing betel. Women seem initially to have favoured this form of consumption, which was common by the early nineteenth century. The areca nut became less important in the quid, as tobacco provided the necessary alkaloid, while astringent *gambir* (cutch) partially replaced the areca taste.[67] Kedu, the main tobacco area in Java with Pekalongan, grew 'Pinang tobacco' at the beginning of the nineteenth century, *pinang* meaning areca in Malay. It was estimated at the time that betel and tobacco together accounted for about a quarter of the daily expenditure of an unmarried commoner in central Java.[68]

Smoking enjoyed a renaissance in Java from the middle of the nineteenth century. For the elite, Manila cigars from the Philippines were all the rage for a time, whereas imported European cigarettes were at first a mere curiosity.[69] For commoners, there were local cigarettes, hand-rolled in leaves. Known as *strootjes* by the Dutch, and *klobot* by the Javanese, they contained admixtures of gums and spices. By far the most successful was the *kretek*, developing from around 1870 in central Java, which consisted of around two parts tobacco to one part chopped cloves, with a sugary 'sauce.' Initially, the industry functioned as a putting-out system, with urban merchants supplying inputs and credit to villagers, and buying their output.[70]

Despite a revival in smoking, betel chewing remained highly significant, in association with tobacco, for example in Aceh.[71] At mid-century, both cigars and betel were exchanged at Sarawak Dayak weddings.[72] Smoking hand-rolled cigarettes, wrapped in banana leaves, was gradually outpacing betel chewing by 1900 in Thailand, and boys as young as five or six were smoking.[73] Combining betel and tobacco in the mouth persisted. Betel chewers placed tobacco and *gambir* together between the teeth and the upper

---

[67] Reid (1985: 535–38) and de Jonge (1988: 92).
[68] Carey (2007: 44, 465–66).
[69] Reid (1985: 538).
[70] Castles (1967).
[71] Penzer (1952: 264–65).
[72] Reid (1985: 540).
[73] Young (1900: 114–15).

lip in western Malaya in the 1830s.[74] In the Philippines, cigars might be chopped up and added to the betel quid.[75] Putting tobacco in a quid was mentioned in a rowing song of 1824 in Thailand and became common across the country in the nineteenth century. In 1864, it was noted that women in Bangkok placed a wad of tobacco between their lips and their upper front teeth, after having chewed a betel quid.[76] In Burma, tobacco and *gambir* were added to the betel quid.[77]

Moreover, men increasingly combined smoking tobacco and chewing betel, by engaging first in one activity, and then in the other. In northeastern Thailand in the early 1880s, men alternated incessantly between smoking and chewing.[78] In Burma, where cheroots were popular, the same system of intermixing smoking and chewing prevailed.[79] In the Philippines, cigars were smoked in parallel with chewing betel in the 1870s.[80] In short, the rise of tobacco in no way spelled the end of betel.

Tobacco Versus Betel in the Twentieth Century

Reid proposes the first half of the twentieth century as a turning point, with cigarettes increasingly replacing betel. Tobacco was grown all over the Dutch East Indies by around 1900, so that it was ubiquitously available.[81] The *kretek* industry also turned into a substantial manufacturing sector, gradually more factory-based and capital-intensive, and importing most cloves from Africa. Owned and operated by Indonesians and 'Foreign Orientals,' this manufacturing sector was geared almost exclusively to the domestic market. From the mid-1920s, European cigarettes were also made in Java, with newly developed Virginia tobacco, competing with *kretek* for local consumers.[82] By the 1930s, Javanese boys as young as three or four years old smoked 'little tapering cigarettes.'[83]

---

[74] Low (1972: 67).
[75] Mertel (2002: 5) citing Jagor (1875).
[76] Reichart and Philipsen (1996: 52–53) and Penzer (1952: 258–59).
[77] Penzer (1952: 255–56) and Thierry (1969: 165).
[78] Reichart and Philipsen (1996: 50–51).
[79] Thierry (1969: 165), Low (1972: 67), and Penzer (1952: 255–56).
[80] Mertel (2002: 5) citing Jagor (1875).
[81] Reid (1985: 531, 536, 538–39).
[82] Castles (1967).
[83] Ponder (1990: 90).

Parallel developments occurred elsewhere in Southeast Asia. In 1909, R. O. Winstedt noted that the 'younger generation' of Malays smoked cigarettes and Burmese cheroots, instead of chewing betel.[84] Thai tobacco was protected by an import tariff from 1926, which encouraged its production as a secondary crop by rice farmers, for the old-fashioned rolling of cigarettes in banana or palm leaves. Western firms then 'tariff-hopped,' as in Indonesia, encouraging the local production of Virginia tobacco, and making Western-style cigarettes in modern factories.[85] The impact of chewing gum, which contains no alkaloids, also needs to be analysed in this context.[86]

However, Reid appears to underestimate the persistence of symbiotic relations between tobacco and betel. In 1925, Collet considered that Sumatran smoking of cigarettes, wrapped in maize leaves, went together with chewing betel, rather than replacing it.[87] The habit of placing a wad of tobacco in the mouth after chewing betel was still widespread in Java in the 1930s.[88] Indeed, this habit has persisted into our own times in both Java and Cambodia.[89] In rural areas of the Philippines, also, tobacco for chewing (*mascada*) remains part of the betel quid and is still widely sold as such in 'wet markets' outside Manila.[90] In Cambodia, cigarette smoking was spreading rapidly in the 1960s, but all markets still sold the ingredients for the betel quid, and all prosperous households had the necessary equipment to hand.[91]

The development of a mass market for cigarettes undermined the status of betel in ritual practices, but not necessarily to the extent that Reid alleges. By the 1930s, cigarettes were being substituted for betel in offerings to the spirits in Kelantan, Malaya, but only when betel was in short supply. The same was true for funerals in Kalimantan and Sulawesi in the 1970s.[92] In Cambodia, tobacco was associated with betel for certain

---

[84] Penzer (1952: 261).
[85] Ingram (1955: 51, 136–41).
[86] Redclift (2006).
[87] Penzer (1952: 265–66).
[88] Ponder (1990: 181).
[89] Gupta and Ray (2004: 32).
[90] Mertel (2002: 6).
[91] Thierry (1969: 7, 230).
[92] Reid (1985: 540).

rituals into the 1960s.[93] And ritual uses of betel persisted into the late twentieth century in Malaya and southern Thailand.[94]

Reid rightly raises the question of gender in these processes, but his answer is unsatisfactory. Women often found themselves excluded from smoking tobacco, at least in public, and Reid notes that they generally gave up betel later than men. He then speculates that they 'appear increasingly to be able to get through the day without such support.'[95] He fails to consider whether they might have turned to stimulants other than betel and tobacco.

Beverages as Competing Substances

A more convincing answer to the riddle of women's experience needs to factor in hot beverages, which are absent from Reid's argument. From the seventeenth century at the latest, such drinks competed with tobacco and betel in Southeast Asia, both as sources of alkaloids, and to cement social relations.

Hot beverages were often present together with betel and tobacco, and there was rarely a linear process of substitution of one substance by another. In the late seventeenth century, people in South Sulawesi chewed betel, took tobacco and drank strong alcohol, sherbet, tea, coffee and chocolate, without any apparent hierarchy in this pattern of consumption.[96] In late nineteenth-century Thailand, it was said that 'every caller is offered a tray of betel-nut and its accompanying condiments; a cup of tea, and cigarettes.'[97] Similarly, Frank Swettenham commented in 1907 that the betel box, passed around after meals in Malaya, was being replaced either with cigarettes or with cups of tea or coffee.[98] In Java, tea and coffee were offered to wedding guests in the 1930s, whereas betel would have been usual earlier.[99]

Tea had been consumed in China since before the Common Era. This was green tea, meaning that leaves were dried immediately after plucking

---

[93] Thierry (1969: 231).
[94] Berlie (1983: 94–98) and Hanks (1968: 126–27).
[95] Reid (1985: 529, 539, 542–43).
[96] Gervaise (1971: 75).
[97] Young (1900: 114). See also p. 90.
[98] Swettenham (1907: 149).
[99] Ponder (1990: 48)

and were not allowed to ferment. The beverage was drunk without milk or sugar.[100] Boiling water provided protection against disease, and tea leaves may initially have been added to flavour this rather insipid drink.[101]

Vietnam, part of China during the first millennium CE, adopted green tea early, while retaining a strong attachment to betel. A Vietnamese proverb declared that 'one can do without tea, but not without betel.'[102] Tea was drunk between meals by 1622 in southern Vietnam, and by grandees in the north towards the end of the century.[103] In the eighteenth century, nobles drank tea in silver or porcelain cups, but the habit was trickling down to more modest social groups. It was offered to guests together with betel.[104] Although tea was cultivated in the Vietnamese highlands by the seventeenth century, imports from China long remained substantial.[105] At the time of the French conquest, smallholders grew green tea essentially for the local market, and it was generally considered inferior to the Chinese article.[106]

Beyond Vietnam, expanding Chinese communities in Southeast Asia were the first consumers of green tea, as locals rarely partook of this beverage as late as the fifteenth century.[107] Chinese voyagers to Southeast Asia at this time remarked that guests were offered betel, not tea.[108] Indeed, mid-nineteenth-century Thailand's annual imports of tea were still attributed mainly to purchases by numerous and entrepreneurial Chinese settlers.[109]

Indigenous peoples gradually took up tea on Chinese lines, especially in Mainland Southeast Asia. Tea was offered to visitors in the Burmese capital as a drink by the 1790s, despite the persistence of chewing tea leaves.[110] In polite circles in the Thai capital, tea was firmly established

[100] Macfarlane and Macfarlane (2003).
[101] Burnett (1999: 18–19).
[102] Thierry (1969: 256).
[103] Dror and Taylor (2006: 118, 234).
[104] Li and Reid (1993: 71, 86, 95, 124).
[105] Nguyen (1965: 84) and Li and Reid (1993: 86, 95).
[106] Bouinais and Paulus (1886: 254).
[107] Reid (1988: 36–45) and Wilson (2000: 1163).
[108] Matsuyama (2003: 200, 270) and Rooney (1993: 5).
[109] Neale (1852: 143, 173).
[110] Symes (1995: 412).

as a necessary civility by the 1680s, although it was said to be 'unknown in all the other places of the kingdom,' and it did not replace betel chewing. Tea was made as an infusion of leaves, without milk or sugar, in small Chinese cups.[111] Tea-pots also became part of Thai royal regalia by the nineteenth century.[112] A go-between in late nineteenth-century Thailand was described as 'sipping her tea' in the course of marriage negotiations, which might earlier have called for betel.[113]

Tea-drinking spread to Maritime Southeast Asia. Javanese and Makassarese were partaking of tea from the seventeenth century, and all classes in Java allegedly consumed it by the early nineteenth century.[114] Notables in southwestern Malaya in the 1830s presented guests with a 'steaming infusion of Souchong, fresh from China,' with no milk or sugar, served in 'minute' cups.[115]

Maritime Southeast Asia experimented more widely with a variety of hot beverages than the Mainland zone. Adding milk and sugar to one's tea became a symbol of pro-European sentiments in early nineteenth-century Java.[116] This was probably a sign that black tea, fermented before drying, or semi-fermented oolong tea, was reaching the region from China by this date, as these kinds of tea are better suited to this form of consumption.

India's indigenous Assam tea, increasingly fermented, certainly became significant from the 1830s.[117] It was successfully introduced in highland Java and Sumatra from the 1870s, after failed attempts to grow East Asian varieties in the framework of the cultivation system.[118] Black or oolong teas then appear to have displaced green tea in Indonesia among the local population, although the balance of preference remains unclear.[119] Dutch planters in the 1930s, faced with ruinous export

---

[111] de la Loubère (1969: 21–22).

[112] Rooney (1993: 12).

[113] Young (1900: 89).

[114] Gervaise (1971: 75), Simmonds (1888: 202), Kumar (1997: 61), and Matsuyama (2003: 245).

[115] Moor (1968: Appendix, 66).

[116] Carey (2007: 180, 663, 718).

[117] Griffiths (1967) and Butel (1989: Ch 5).

[118] Etherington (1974: 84–88), Matsuyama (2003: 271–72), Deuss (1913: 1–3), and Ibbetson (1925: 50).

[119] Etherington (1974: 85–86) and Matsuyama (2003: 272).

conditions, made great efforts to popularize their tea among Javanese 'natives,' using vans equipped with loudspeakers, colourful posters and local agents.[120]

Arabica coffee was an Ethiopian plant, and its cultivation spread from Yemen to western India in the early seventeenth century, and thence to Java and beyond.[121] Reid opines that coffee drinking only spread in the eighteenth century, as a consequence of cultivation in Java, but it was already drunk by 1667.[122] In 1733, West Javanese regents, obliged to grow coffee for export for the Dutch East India Company, were 'allowed to keep a small garden within their compounds for private consumption.'[123] By 1830, coffee was even described as a 'traditional' drink of Javanese peasants.[124] In 1824, elite Makassarese in South Sulawesi served coffee.[125] Ternate, in Maluku, had to import coffee for local consumption in 1846. A decade later, the little island produced about 100 *pikul*, or 6 metric tons, entirely for its own needs.[126] Madura imported 30 tons in 1936.[127]

Indeed, the role of coffee as the most lucrative export crop in Indonesia's infamous 'cultivation system' has obscured the significance of the beverage for local consumption. In the 1870s, the *Ceylon Directory* estimated that 20,000 tons, or just under 20% of Indonesia's harvest, was for local use.[128] Government coffee auctions in Java in 1869–1870, intended to serve the colony's own requirements, amounted to just over 3000 tons a year, but this was clearly much lower than actual consumption.[129] After coffee rust (*Hemileia vastatrix*) devastated Arabica groves from the 1870s, Robusta varieties were introduced, and the internal market continued to grow.[130] By 1928, it was officially estimated that Java

---

[120] Ponder (1990: 75–77).
[121] Clarence-Smith (2001).
[122] Reid (1988: 36) and Simmonds (1888: 202).
[123] Remmelink (1994: 71–72).
[124] Elson (1994: 7).
[125] Olivier (1834–1837: II, 214).
[126] ANRI, 31, 167 'Register der aantekeningen van de kommissaris voor Menado, 1846'; ANRI, 52, 1657, 'Beknopt overzicht, Buiten-Bezittingen, 1855.'
[127] de Jonge (1988: 71).
[128] Thurber (1881: 240).
[129] ANRI, 52, 1659, 'Kultuur verslag, Java, 1870.'
[130] Clarence-Smith (2003).

consumed 28,000 tons a year, and the rest of Indonesia 10,500 tons.[131] Local drinking was said to take up about a third of Indonesia's total output in the 1930s, higher than for any other staple export crop of the colony, and in 1939 this reached 42%.[132] In the 1930s, coffee was considered to be the most popular beverage in Java, usually drunk black in Turkish style. It was often unsweetened, perhaps reflecting the cost of sugar rather than established tastes.[133]

Elsewhere in the region, coffee had a more modest following. A visitor to Manila complained in 1796 that coffee was completely unobtainable.[134] A little coffee was available by the 1870s, but an export boom, from the 1850s to the 1880s, did surprisingly little to make the beverage popular internally, despite the crop's excellent quality.[135] Coffee only really took off after 1898, when the Americans took over the Philippines.[136] Malaya experienced a brief planting boom from the 1870s to the 1890s, and some coffee was locally consumed. Although Malaya became a net importer in the early 1920s, coffee remained subordinate to tea.[137] Burma's consumption of coffee went back to the late eighteenth century and also necessitated imports, but on a minor scale.[138] Thailand produced a little for internal market from the 1890s.[139] French cultural habits raised consumption slightly in Indochina, but on a minor scale.[140]

Chocolate (*Theobroma cacao*), a drink rather than a snack till the late nineteenth century, was an alkaloid-bearing beverage from the New World introduced by Europeans, who also transferred seedlings from the mid-seventeenth century.[141] Cultivation took root in Dutch Sri Lanka and the Spanish Philippines, diffusing to Java in the eighteenth century, and then to eastern Indonesia. In 1824, elite Makassarese in

---

[131] Creutzberg (1975: 100).
[132] Ultée (1946–1950: 17).
[133] Ponder (1990: 62, 77, 92, 227) and Matsuyama (2003: 244–45, 253, 270).
[134] Zaide and Zaide (1990: VI, 245).
[135] González Fernández (1875: 64, 107–8, 114) and Mallat (1983: 123, 156, 169).
[136] Miller (1920: 77, 174, 289, 470).
[137] Lewin (1924: 202), Gullick (1988: 112), and Jackson (1968).
[138] Sangermano (1966: 218) and Haarer (1956: 375).
[139] Donner (1978: 494–95).
[140] Robequain (1944: 197).
[141] Coe and Michael (1996) and Clarence-Smith (2000).

South Sulawesi served chocolate together with coffee. However, it was only in the Philippines that drinking chocolate really took root, on Mesoamerican and Spanish lines, gradually penetrating well down the social scale.[142]

Religious Factors Favouring Hot Beverages Over Tobacco and Betel

Reid fails to explore religion properly in his account, and yet expanding world faiths generally championed hot beverages, while often frowning on tobacco and betel. Clerical groups were among the foremost pioneers of hot beverages around the globe, and the geographical distribution of proselytizing faiths correlated fairly well with the spread of particular beverages.[143] Loubère, a seventeenth-century French missionary, associated coffee with 'Moors,' tea with the Thai and Chinese, and chocolate with the Portuguese.[144]

Proselytizing religious groups concentrated on attacking products such as opium and 'demon alcohol,' and their support for hot beverages was largely indirect.[145] Nevertheless, drinking such substances was associated with a spiritually and socially elevated lifestyle. Consumption slowly trickled down to the masses, providing alkaloids that were acceptable substitutes for those from betel, and superior to tobacco. Furthermore, women, who were excluded from smoking tobacco, could partake of such beverages.

Both China's tea habit and the cultivation of the tree spread in the first millennium CE.[146] In areas of the 'East Asian religious synthesis,' green tea reigned supreme, for it was Mahayana Buddhist monks' aid to meditation, Daoists' 'elixir of life,' and an integral part of Confucian public rites.[147] Indeed, Buddhist monks saved tea in Korea, after rulers and aristocrats had turned to alcohol and commoners to cereal-based

---

[142] Clarence-Smith (1998). For Makassar, Olivier (1834–1837: II, 214).

[143] Clarence-Smith (2008).

[144] de la Loubère (1969: 22–23).

[145] Evans (1992: 33), Macfarlane and Macfarlane (2003: 39), and Lane (1986: 345).

[146] Macfarlane and Macfarlane (2003), Gardella (1994), Butel (1989), and Evans (1992).

[147] Macfarlane and Macfarlane (2003: 44), Evans (1992: 20), and Wang (2000: 52–68).

beverages.[148] That green tea should have predominated in Vietnam thus made eminent sense.

Theravada Buddhism, rooted in Sri Lanka, similarly helped to make green tea the hot beverage of choice in the rest of Mainland Southeast Asia. Monks were again to the fore, with Thai monks drinking tea, presumably as an aid to meditation.[149]

Chocolate was famously beloved of Catholic clerics, whereas coffee and tea were more prized among their Protestant rivals.[150] Given the influence of the Catholic church in the Philippines, it is scarcely surprising that priests and friars popularized both the beverage and the cultivation of the crop.[151] However, the beverage was also popular in the 1810s in the Islamic southwest of the Philippines, perhaps because the numerous Catholic Filipino slaves passed on the habit to their owners.[152] Chocolate also had a foothold in Indonesia, especially in eastern regions where Islam, Protestantism and Animism co-existed.[153]

Coffee and tea have historically battled for the allegiance of Muslims. Coffee developed an early association with Sufi mystics and then more generally with the ulama.[154] However, tea spread from either end of the Dar al-Islam from the seventeenth century, into Inner Asia and Persia, on the one hand, and into Morocco and the western Maghrib, on the other.[155]

In Southeast Asia, coffee has sometimes been designated as an Islamic drink.[156] Thus, the affection for coffee currently shown by Cham communities of Vietnam and Cambodia may reflect their Islamic identity, helping to demarcate them culturally from tea-drinking Vietnamese.[157] That said, Arab communities migrating to Southeast Asia have been

---

[148] Anthony (1997) and Butel (1989: 32–33).
[149] Young (1900: 261).
[150] Clarence-Smith (2000), Schivelbusch (1992), and Harwich (1992).
[151] Stols (1996: 44).
[152] Moor (1968: 39–40, 44, 50) and Burbidge (1989: 221).
[153] Clarence-Smith (1998).
[154] Hattox (1985).
[155] Matthee (2005), Butel (1989: 217, 225–26, 231–33), and Griffiths (1967: 11–13).
[156] Clarence-Smith (2001).
[157] Taylor (2007: 32, 40, 84, 144–45, 153, 246).

credited with tipping the balance from coffee to Javanese oolong tea in their homeland of Hadhramaut (East Yemen).[158]

Conversely, betel remained popular in areas where proselytizing world religions made few inroads. Thus, betel retains a strong following in Animist zones, such as highland Malaya and eastern Indonesia.[159] (With regard to the latter area, it is probable that betel would have been present in bride-wealth rituals that involved the giving and receiving of art objects, see Michael North chapter in this volume.) That said, Taiwan's striking revival in betel consumption in the latter half of the twentieth century is somewhat puzzling.[160] Similarly, South Asia remains much addicted to betel, in both Hindu and Muslim zones.[161]

Religions could also affect consumption by prohibiting certain substances. In this regard, Reid wrongly states that there was no Islamic opposition to tobacco.[162] In late-seventeenth century Banten, a famous centre of Islamic fervour, the ulama 'prohibited opium and tobacco smoking,' possibly because the two were so closely intertwined. Even more strikingly, Tuanku Nan Rinceh, one of the main Padri Islamic reformers in early nineteenth-century West Sumatra, reportedly killed his own aunt for consuming tobacco. Inspired by the puritanical Wahhabi of Arabia, who banned all substances analogous to wine, the Padris forced their followers to abjure tobacco, opium and alcohol. However, the fall of the first Wahhabi regime, in the late 1810s, coincided with a declining Padri fervour in banning tobacco.[163] The al-Qadri ruling family of Pontianak, West Kalimantan, who were reforming Arab descendants of the Prophet, abjured both opium and tobacco around 1800.[164]

To be sure, Islamic reformers in other parts of the globe, occasionally pronounced tea and coffee to be forbidden to the faithful, by analogy with wine.[165] Indeed, the question of the acceptability of coffee led to one of the great religious controversies that shook early Islam.[166]

---

[158] van der Meulen (1947: 148).
[159] Penzer (1952: 259–60) and Roger Montgomery, personal communication.
[160] Gupta and Ray (2004: 31–32) and Parsell (2005).
[161] Jana (2006: 31, 38).
[162] Reid (1985: 540).
[163] Dobbin (1983: 132, 146, 174).
[164] Moor (1968: Appendix, 11).
[165] Matthee (2005), Lane (1986: 346), and Bemath (1992: 41, 43).
[166] Hattox (1985).

However, there is no evidence that condemnations of these beverages spilled over into Islamic Southeast Asia. Darul Islam guerrillas anathemized chocolate in South Sulawesi in 1953, but seemingly as a luxury foodstuff rather than as a stimulant.[167]

In Mainland Southeast Asia, Theravada Buddhist monks were not meant to smoke tobacco or drink alcohol.[168] Monastic rules did not bind the laity, but acted as markers of superior morality. Thai and Burmese rulers avoided consuming alcohol in public and occasionally prohibited its use. Pious Theravada Buddhists may voluntarily have shunned it.[169] It is unclear whether this sensitivity extended to tobacco, and the ban on monastic smoking was little enforced in late nineteenth-century Thailand.[170] Vietnam was perhaps the most tolerant part of Southeast Asia, although Mahayana Buddhist attitudes remain to be explored.[171]

In contrast, betel chewing never appears to have been the subject of religious sanction in Mainland Southeast Asia. The practice extended to encompass some Tibetan Buddhist monasteries.[172] Indeed, Theravada Buddhist monks were almost encouraged to chew betel, for it was considered to be a great stimulator of meditative faculties.[173]

Although an Islamic tradition held that betel should not be chewed in the hours of daylight during the month of fasting, treating it as a kind of food, Muslims generally tolerated the stimulant.[174] Indeed, in 1682 it was reported that Shaykh Yusuf al-Makassari was 'revered as a saint by many of the Muslims in Batavia, who collected his *sepah* (chewed betel nut) from the ground and treated it as a holy relic.'[175] In the mid-eighteenth century, a holy man of East Java cured the ruler of Balambangan's daughter by making her chew a betel nut.[176]

---

[167] Boland (1982: 66).
[168] Thierry (1969: 166–67), Reichart and Philipsen (1996: 25), and Penzer (1952: 256).
[169] Reid (1988: 40), Lieberman (2003: 175, 196–97), Sangermano (1966: 160), and de la Loubère (1969: 22–23).
[170] Young (1900: 261).
[171] Dror and Taylor (2006: 118), for rice wine.
[172] Penzer (1952: 202) and Maraini (1952: 87).
[173] Reichart and Philipsen (1996: 25), Penzer (1952: 256), and Thierry (1969: 166–67, 233).
[174] Gode (1961: I, 125).
[175] Ward (2009: 205).
[176] Ricklefs (1993: 10).

That said, the Padri Muslim reformers of West Sumatra prohibited betel after 1803, along with tobacco, alcohol and opium, albeit with indifferent success.[177] Similarly, the al-Qadri *sayyid* clan of Pontianak refused to chew betel around 1800, and the religious prestige of these descendants of the Prophet was considerable.[178] There is even a suggestion that the word *abangan,* meaning 'the red group,' a term applied in Java by pious Muslims to adherents of syncretic Javanism, reflected the red-stained lips of their betel-chewing opponents.[179]

CONCLUSION

There was no single cause for changes in the consumption of betel and tobacco, but Tony Reid, in his stimulating and seminal article, neglected the intimately intertwined roles of religion and hot beverages, notably in the context of women's experiences. While cigarettes were beneficiaries of the decline of betel, this was true mainly of masculine consumption. For women, hot beverages were better placed than tobacco to substitute for betel. With such beverages popularized by world religions, secular reformers were in a better position to launch campaigns against betel.

There remains a historical puzzle concerning the sudden collapse in the popularity of betel. A custom that was addictive, and that had become deeply entrenched in local culture over millennia, all but vanished with remarkable speed, at least in parts of Southeast Asia. The region is the presumed historical cradle of betel, which makes it all the more surprising that its inhabitants should abandon a habit that reached into almost every nook and cranny of their lives. Adding to the mystery, the physical act of mastication yields a particular type of pleasure, which cannot be substituted by smoking or drinking.

The decline of betel is all the more surprising, because taste is among the most conservative of the senses. Olfactory and gustatory processes together govern how human beings assess what they place in their mouths, and memory defends against poisoning.[180] Once learned, preferences are hard to change, and taste stirs deep emotions, as in Marcel

---

[177] Dobbin (1983: 132, 146) and Reid (1985: 539).
[178] Moor (1968: Appendix, 11).
[179] Ricklefs (2007: 86).
[180] Blake (2006).

Proust's famous story of the *madeleine*. However, changing social and cultural attitudes can lead to sudden alterations, and the story of betel may point to the later fate of tobacco.

BIBLIOGRAPHY

ANRI = Arsip Nasional Republik Indonesia (Jakarta), Residency Archives.
Anthony, Brother. 1997. A Short History of Tea. *Transactions of the Korea branch of the Royal Asiatic Society* 72: 1–11.
Barr, Andrew. 1998. *Drink: A Social History*. London: Pimlico.
Bemath, Abdul S. 1992. The Sayyid and Saalihiya Tariga: Reformist Anticolonial Hero in Somalia. In *In the Shadow of Conquest: Islam in Colonial Northeast Africa*, ed. Said S. Samatar, 33–47. Trenton: Red Sea Press.
Berlie, Jean. 1983. *Tepi Laut, un Village Malais au Bord de la mer*. Paris: Editions de la Maisnie.
Bigalke, Terance W. 2005. *Tana Toraja: A Social History of an Indonesian People*. Singapore: Singapore University Press.
Blake, Anthony. 2006. The Learning of Human Flavour Preferences. In *Flavour in Food*, ed. A. Voilley and P. Etiévant, 369–402. Cambridge: Woodhead.
Boland, B.J. 1982. *The Struggle of Islam in Modern Indonesia*, 2nd ed. The Hague: M. Nijhoff.
Bouinais, A., and A. Paulus. 1886. *La France en Indochine*. Paris: Challamel Aîné.
Burbidge, F.W. 1989. *The Gardens of the Sun, a Naturalist's Journal of Borneo and the Sulu Archipelago*. Singapore: Oxford University Press.
Burnett, John. 1999. *Liquid Pleasures, a Social History of Drinks in Modern Britain*. London: Routledge.
Butel, Paul. 1989. *Histoire du thé*. Paris: Éditions Desjonquères.
Carey, Peter. 2007. *The Power of Prophecy: Prince Dipanagara and the End of an Old Order in Java, 1785–1855*. Leiden: KITLV Press.
Castles, Lance. 1967. *Religion, Politics and Economic Behaviour in Java: The Kudus Cigarette Industry*. New Haven: Yale University Southeast Asian Studies.
Clarence-Smith, William G. 1998. The Rise and Fall of Maluku Cocoa Production in the Nineteenth Century: Lessons for the Present. In *Old World Places, New World Problems: Exploring Resource Management Issues in Eastern Indonesia*, ed. S. Pannell and F. von Benda-Beckmann, 113–142. Canberra: Centre for Resource and Environmental Studies.
Clarence-Smith, William G. 2000. *Cocoa and Chocolate, 1765–1914*. London: Routledge.
Clarence-Smith, William G. 2001. The Spread of Coffee Cultivation in Asia, from the Seventeenth to the Early Nineteenth Century. In *Le commerce du café avant l'ère des plantations coloniales*, ed. Michel Tuchscherer, 371–384. Cairo: Institut Français d'Archéologie Orientale.

Clarence-Smith, William G. 2003. The Coffee Crisis in Asia, Africa and the Pacific, 1870–1914. In *The Global Coffee Economy in Africa, Asia and Latin America, 1500–1989*, ed. William G. Clarence-Smith and Steven Topik, 100–119. Cambridge: Cambridge University Press.

Clarence-Smith, William G. 2008. The Global Consumption of Hot Beverages, c. 1500 to c. 1900. In *Food and Globalization: Consumption, Markets and Politics in the Modern World*, ed. Alexander Nützenadel and Frank Trentmann, 37–55. Oxford: Berg.

Coe, Sophie D., and D. Michael. 1996. *The True History of Chocolate*. London: Thames and Hudson.

Creutzberg, P. 1975. *Indonesia's Export Crops, 1816–1940*. The Hague: M. Nijhoff (Volume 1 of *Changing Economy in Indonesia*).

de Jesus, Edilberto C. 1980. *The Tobacco Monopoly in the Philippines: Bureaucratic Enterprise and Social Change, 1766–1880*. Manila: Ateneo de Manila Press.

de Jesus, Edilberto C. 1982. Control and Compromise in the Cagayan Valley. In *Philippine Social History: Global Trade and Local Transformations*, ed. Alfred W. McCoy and Edilberto de Jesus, 21–37. New Haven, CT: Yale University.

de Jonge, Huub. 1988. *Handelaren en handlangers: Ondernemerschap, economische ontwikkeling en Islam op Madura*. Dordrecht: Foris.

de la Loubère, Simon. 1969. *The Kingdom of Siam*. Kuala Lumpur: Oxford University Press (reprint of 1693 ed.).

Deuss, J.J.B. 1913. *De theecultuur*. Haarlem: H.D. Tjeenk Willink & Zoon.

Dikötter, Frank, Lars Laamann, and Xun Zhou. 2004. *Narcotic Culture: A History of Drugs in China*. London: Hurst.

Dobbin, Christine. 1983. *Islamic Revivalism in a Changing Peasant Economy: Central Sumatra 1784–1847*. London: Curzon.

Donner, Wolf. 1978. *The Five Faces of Thailand*. London: C. Hurst.

Dror, Olga, and Keith W. Taylor. 2006. *Views of Seventeenth-Century Vietnam: Christoforo Borri on Cochinchina and Samuel Baron on Tonkin*. Ithaca: Cornell University.

Elson, R.E. 1994. *Village Java Under the Cultivation System, 1830–1870*. Sydney: Allen and Unwin.

Etherington, D.M. 1974. The Indonesian Tea Industry. *Bulletin of Indonesian Economic Studies* 10 (2): 83–113.

Evans, John C. 1992. *Tea in China: The History of China's National Drink*. New York: Greenwood.

Galvão, António. 1971. *A treatise on the Moluccas (c. 1544), probably the preliminary version of António Galvão's lost História das Molucas*, ed. and trans. S.J. Hubert Jacobs. Rome: Jesuit Historical Institute.

Gardella, Robert. 1994. *Harvesting Mountains: Fujian and the China Tea Trade, 1757–1937*. Berkeley: University of California Press.

Gervaise, Nicolas. 1971. *An Historical Description of the Kingdom of Macasar in the East Indies*. Westmead: Gregg International (reprint of 1701 ed.).
Gode, P.K. 1961. *Studies in Indian Cultural History*, vol. 1. Poona: Publication Committee.
González Fernández, R. 1875. *Manual del viajero en Filipinas*. Manila: Tip. de Santo Tomás.
Goodman, Jordan. 1993. *Tobacco in History: The Cultures of Dependence*. London: Routledge.
Goodman, Jordan, Paul Lovejoy, and Anrew Sherratt (eds.). 1995. *Consuming Habits, Drugs in History and Anthropology*. London: Routledge.
Griffiths, Percival J. 1967. *The History of the Indian Tea Industry*. London: Weidenfeld and Nicolson.
Gullick, John M. 1988. *Kuala Lumpur 1880–1895, a City in the Making*. Selangor: Pelanduk Publications.
Gupta, P.C., and C.S. Ray. 2004. Epedimiology of Betel Quid Usage. *Annals of the Academy of Medicine (Singapore)* 33 (Suppl., 4): 31–36.
Haarer, A.E. 1956. *Modern Coffee Production*. London: L. Hill.
Hanks, Jane R. 1968. *Maternity and Its Rituals in Bang Chan*, 2nd printing. Ithaca: Cornell University.
Harwich, Nikita. 1992. *Histoire du chocolat*. Paris: Éditions Desjonquères.
Hattox, Ralph S. 1985. *Coffee and Coffeehouses: The Origins of a Social Beverage in the Medieval Near East*. Seattle: University of Washington Press.
Hesse, Manfred. 2002. *Alkaloids: Nature's Curse or Blessing?*. New York: Wiley.
Ibbetson, A.C. 1925. *Tea, from Grower to Consumer*. London: Pitman.
Ingram, James C. 1955. *Economic Change in Thailand Since 1850*. Stanford: Stanford University Press.
Jackson, James C. 1968. *Planters and Speculators: Chinese and European Agricultural Enterprises in Malaya, 1786–1921*. Kuala Lumpur: University of Malaya Press.
Jagor, F. 1875. *Travels in the Philippines*. London: Chapman & Hall.
Jana, B.L. 2006. *Betelvine: A Traditional Cash Crop of Rural India*. Udaipur: Agrotech Publications Academy.
Kumar, Ann. 1997. *Java and Modern Europe: Ambiguous Encounters*. Richmond: Curzon.
Lane, Edward W. 1986. *An Account of the Manners and Customs of the Modern Egyptians*. London: Darf (reprint of 1896 ed.).
Lewin, Evans. 1924. *The Resources of the Empire and Their Development*. London: W. Collins Sons & Co.
Li, Tana, and Anthony Reid, comps. 1993. *Southern Vietnam Under the Nguyen: Documents on the Economic History of Cochinchina (Dang Trong), 1602–1777*. Singapore: Institute of Southeast Asian Studies.

Lieberman, Victor. 2003. *Strange Parallels: Southeast Asia in Global Context C. 800–1830: Volume 1, Integration on the Mainland*. Cambridge: Cambridge University Press.
Loureiro, Rui M. 2007. "*A verde folha da erva ardente*": Betel Chewing in Sixteenth-Century European Sources. *Review of Culture* 21: 49–63.
Low, James. 1972. *The British Settlement of Penang*. Singapore: Oxford University Press (reprint of 1836 ed.).
Macfarlane, Alan, and Iris Macfarlane. 2003. *Green Gold: The Empire of Tea*. London: Ebury Press.
Macmillan, H.F. 1925. *Tropical Gardening and Planting, with Special Reference to Ceylon*. Colombo: Times of Ceylon.
Mallat, Jean. 1983. *The Philippines: History, Geography, Customs, Agriculture, Industry and Commerce of the Spanish Colonies in Oceania*, trans. French ed. Manila: National Historical Institute.
Maraini, Fosco. 1952. *Secret Tibet*. London: Hutchinson.
Matsuyama, Akira. 2003. *The Traditional Dietary Culture of South East Asia: Its Formation and Pedigree*. London: Kegan Paul.
Matthee, Rudi. 2005. *The Pursuit of Pleasure: Drugs and Stimulants in Iranian History, 1500–1900*. Princeton: Princeton University Press.
Mertel, Timothy. 2002. Betel Chewing in the Philippines. *L'Asie exotique*. http://www.lasieexotique.com/mag_betel.html.
Miller, Hugo H. 1920. *Economic Conditions in the Philippines*. Boston: Ginn & Co.
Moor, J.H. (ed.). 1968. *Notices of the Indian Archipelago and Adjacent Countries*. London: Frank Cass (reprint of 1837 ed.).
Neale, Fred A. 1852. *Narrative of a Residence at the Capital of the Kingdom of Siam*. London: Office of the National Illustrated Library.
Nguyen, Thanh Nha. 1965. *Tableau économique du Vietnam aux XVIIe et XVIIIe siècles*. Paris: Bibliothèque Bich-Thanh-Thu.
Nguyen, Xuan-hien, and P.A. Reichart. 2008. Betel-Chewing in Mainland Southeast Asia. *IAAS Newsletter* 47: 26–27.
Olivier, J. 1834–1837. *Reizen in den Molukschen archipel naar Makassar en z., in het gevolg van den Gouverneur-Generaal van Nederlandsch-Indië*. Amsterdam: G.J.A. Beijerinck.
Parsell, Diana. 2005. Palm Nut Problem: Asian Chewing Habit Linked to Oral Cancer. *Science News Online*. http://www.sciencenews.org/articles/20050115/bob10.asp.
Penzer, N.M. 1952. *Poison-Damsels and Other Essays in Folklore and Anthropology*. London: Chas. J. Sawyer Ltd. (privately printed).
Ponder, H.W. 1990. *Javanese Panorama: More Impressions of the 1930s*. Singapore: Oxford University Press.

Redclift, Michael R. 2006. Chewing Gum: Mass Consumption and the "Shadow-Lands" of the Yucatán. In *Consuming Cultures, Global Perspectives, Historical Trajectories, Transnational Exchanges*, ed. John Brewer and Frank Trentmann, 167–188. Oxford: Berg.
Reichart, Peter, and Hans P. Philipsen. 1996. *Betel and Miang: Vanishing Thai Habits*. Bangkok: White Lotus.
Reid, Anthony. 1985. From Betel-Chewing to Tobacco-Smoking in Indonesia. *Journal of Asian Studies* 44 (3): 529–547.
Reid, Anthony. 1988. *Southeast Asia in the Age of Commerce, 1450–1680, Volume 1, the Lands Below the Winds*. New Haven: Yale University Press.
Reid, Anthony. 1992. Economic and Social Change. In *The Cambridge History of Southeast Asia, Volume One, from Early Times to c. 1800*, ed. Nicholas Tarling, 460–507. Cambridge: Cambridge University Press.
Remmelink, Willem. 1994. *The Chinese War and the Collapse of the Javanese State, 1727–1743*. Leiden: KITLV Press.
Ricklefs, M.C. 1993. *A History of Modern Indonesia Since c. 1300*, 2nd ed. London: Macmillan.
Ricklefs, M.C. 2007. *Polarizing Javanese Society, Islamic and Other Visions, 1830–1930*. Honolulu: University of Hawai'i Press.
Robequain, Charles. 1944. *The Economic Development of French Indochina*. London: Oxford University Press.
Rooney, Dawn F. 1993. *Betel Chewing Traditions in South-East Asia*. Kuala Lumpur: Oxford University Press.
Sangermano, [Vicentius]. 1966. *A Description of the Burmese Empire*. London: Susil Gupta.
Schivelbusch, Wolfgang. 1992. *Tastes of Paradise, a Social History of Spices, Stimulants and Intoxicants*. New York: Pantheon Books.
Simmonds, P.L. 1888. *The Popular Beverages of Various Countries*. London: J.G. Smith.
Stols, Eddy. 1996. Le cacao: Le sang voluptueux du nouveau monde. In *Chocolat, de la boisson élitaire au bâton populaire*, ed. Emmanuel Collet, 37–56. Brussels: CGER.
Swettenham, Frank A. 1907. *British Malaya, an Account of the Origin and Progress of British Influence in Malaya*. London: John Lane, The Bodley Head.
Symes, Michael. 1995. *An Account of an Embassy to the Kingdom of Ava in the Year 1795*. New Delhi: Asian Educational Services (reprint of 1800 ed.).
Taylor, Philip. 2007. *Muslims of the Mekong Delta: Place and Mobility in the Cosmopolitan Periphery*. Copenhagen: NIAS Press.
Thierry, Solange. 1969. *Le bétel, I, Inde et Asie du Sud-Est*. Paris: Muséum National d'Histoire Naturelle.

Thurber, Francis B. 1881. *Coffee, from Plantation to Cup.* New York: American Grocer Association.
Ultée, A.J. 1946–1950. Koffiecultuur der ondernemingen. In *De landbouw in de Indische archipel,* vol. 2 b, ed. C.J.J. van Hall and C. van de Koppel, 7–88. The Hague: W. van Hoeve.
van der Meulen, D. 1947. *Aden to Hadhramaut: A Journey in South Arabia.* London: John Murray.
Wang, Ling. 2000. *Chinese Tea Culture.* Beijing: Foreign Languages Press.
Ward, Kerry. 2009. *Networks of Empire: Forced Migration in the Dutch East India Company.* Cambridge: Cambridge University Press.
Wilson, C.S. 2000. Southeast Asia. In *The Cambridge World History of Food,* ed. Kenneth F. Kiple and Kriemhild Conèe Ornelas. Cambridge: Cambridge University Press.
Wyatt, David K. 1982. *Thailand, a Short History.* New Haven: Yale University Press.
Young, Ernest. 1900. *The Kingdom of the Yellow Robe.* London: Archibald Constable.
Zaide, Gregorio, and Sonia Zaide, eds. 1990. *Documentary Sources of Philippine History.* Manila: National Book Store.

Domestic Interiors in Seventeenth- and Eighteenth-Century Batavia

Michael North

Abstract This chapter focuses on the interior decoration of seventeenth- and eighteenth-century Batavia homes. On the basis of probate inventories, I'll try to shed a special light on the households of non-Dutch people, such as the Chinese and the Muslim population. While Dutch families appear to have incorporated Asian decorative objects from the beginning, a greater exchange between Western and indigenous patterns in Chinese and Asian households seems to have been taken place only in the eighteenth centuries to a larger extent. In the following, I shall reconstruct facets of domestic interior decoration and answer the question to what extent the different ethnic groups accommodated specific styles and furnishings.

Keywords Batavia · Dutch East India Company (VOC) · Domestic interior decoration · Chinese · Muslims

M. North (✉)
University of Greifswald, Greifswald, Germany

© The Author(s) 2019
R. A. G. Reyes (ed.), *Art, Trade, and Cultural Mediation in Asia, 1600–1950*, https://doi.org/10.1057/978-1-137-57237-0_5

INTRODUCTION

In 1619, the new Governor General Jan Pietersz Coen of the Verenigde Oost-Indische Compagnie (VOC) founded the fort of Batavia as a headquarters of the VOC in Asia which overtook the responsibility for all Company activities in the region. Batavia replaced the existing town, Jacatra, which had been a meeting place for Dutch ships and Chinese junks since the first Dutch fleet (under the command of Cornelius de Houtmans reached Java in 1595). Dutch ships sailing to the Moluccas, called at Jacatra for provisions and Chinese, Dutch and English merchants settled there. The merchants of the English East India Company were trying to gain land in Jacatra, Jan Piersz. Coen instead took control over this city. As Jacatra, Batavia was multiethnic and multicultural from the beginning.

The Dutch part of the population consisted of Company servants and so-called freeburghers, who were often former Company personnel. The men in this population either cohabited with indigenous concubines or else took Asian wives. Although towards the end of the seventeenth century, the upper echelons of Dutch society succeeded in marrying European women, in the long run the number of available Dutch women decreased. As a consequence, the frequency of marriages between Dutch men and Asian or Eurasian women rose, leading over the course of the eighteenth century to a significant increase in the number of descendants of Eurasian or Indoasian parentage.[1]

The Chinese, who outnumbered the Europeans, fell into several categories. There were merchants who had settled in Jacatra before the Dutch came. Then there were Chinese craftsmen who were brought to Batavia to satisfy local demand for their skills. Furthermore, Chinese landowners played a crucial role in sugar production. The sizeable group of Mardijkers were Europeanised Christian ex-slaves of Bengal or Tamil origin. Most of them had been freed by the Portuguese; they bore Portuguese names and spoke that language. Others had been given Dutch names on the occasion of their baptism. As a general rule, Mardijkers tended to marry into Eurasian families. An important component of Batavian society was formed by free Asian groups such as the Bandanese or the Balinese, who served as auxiliary troops in Dutch military campaigns. The Malay formed a closed group of Muslim

---

[1] U. Bosma and R. Raben, *Being "Dutch" in the Indies: A History of Creolisation and Empire, 1500–1920* (Singapore, 2008), 33–38.

traders and shipowners. They were related to the "Moren" (Moors), a term applied to Muslims, often of Tamil origin, who had arrived from Southern India. Members of all these groups owned land in the surroundings of Batavia, with the Dutch and a few Chinese occupying the manor estates. The Dutch and the Chinese—but also Mardijkers and traders from the free Asian population—competed in the slave trade, importing slaves from the Indian Ocean littoral and around the Indonesian Archipelago to Batavia. Only a small number was owned by the VOC; in fact most slaves were privately owned, even by modest Chinese households. One can easily imagine that they formed a sizeable proportion of Batavia's population.[2] In the following, I shall reconstruct facets of domestic interior decoration and answer the question to what extent the different ethnic groups accommodated specific styles and furnishings.

Sources

The most significant sources touching the possession of art objects and material goods in colonial households are the so-called probate inventories, registrations of the movables left behind by a deceased person. These inventories were kept by the orphanage or *weeskamer*. Several probate inventories from the *weeskamer* in Batavia can be studied in copies deposited in various Dutch archives. The majority, however, were drawn up for other courts, the estate chamber (*boedelkamer*) and the aldermen's court (*schepenbank*). These documents are preserved in the National Archives of Indonesia (Arsip Nasional) in Jakarta, where only some of them are presently accessible.

Unfortunately, the surviving inventories are not as detailed as those from the Golden Age of the Dutch Republic. They seldom specify the subjects of paintings and as a rule do not mention attributes or motifs. Moreover, due to their inferior state of conservation, poorer rate of survival and different storage conditions, the Batavia inventories do not lend themselves as well as Dutch inventories to quantitative and statistical analysis. Still, they yield qualitative and quantitative evidence on the art objects owned in colonial households.

[2] Ibid., 37–89; E. Niemeijer, *Calvinisme en koloniale stadscultuur, Batavia 1619–1725* (Amsterdam, 1996), 26. See also J. Gellman Taylor, *The Social World of Batavia: Europeans and Eurasians in Colonial Indonesia*. New Perspectives in SE Asian Studies (Madison, 2009).

"Dutch" Houses and Decoration

In terms of urban planning and layout for fortifications, canals, drawbridges, etc., Batavia very much resembles the Dutch prototype, reinforced not least by the fact that engineers, masons, and even building materials (brick) had been imported from Europe. But actual building design and architecture differed visibly from the Netherlands. In Batavia, the outer wall of buildings were plastered to protect the bricks from heat, heavy rain and corrosion characteristic of a tropical climate; roof ridges were constructed parallel (and not perpendicular as in Europe) to the street to facilitate flow-off and drainage during heavy rains; and broad overhangs were erected at the front and the back of houses to protect the entrances from sun, heat and tropical storms. The creators of this "Indische" architectural design were also representatives of a new type of domestic culture: the Dutch houseowners and their indigenous concubines (nyai), helped by their Chinese overseers (mandor), and Chinese and Javanese workers.[3]

Inside the house, Dutch objects prevailed, but the Europeans also bought and displayed Asian cultural goods such as notably porcelain, lanterns, lacquerware, artefacts and paintings. With reference to the private ownership of art in colonial households, the aforementioned probate inventories certainly serve as a principal source, but due to incomplete documentation and research for the case of Batavia, a fuller and more detailed picture of distinctly "Asian" inventories is still wanting and in any case remains difficult to quantify. Still, there are some known art collections collated and amassed by the Dutch company (VOC) servants. For example, in 1647, the court master of the Governor General, van Heck, left behind three portraits of members of the House of Orange, four allegories on the four-seasons and three landscape paintings.[4]

Already in the 1620s, Gillis Vinant, a merchant and burgher of Batavia, had amassed an impressive collection of paintings. Twenty-eight

---

[3] See Peter J. M. Nas, "'Indische' Architecture in Indonesia," in T. DaCosta Kaufmann and M. North, ed., *Mediating Netherlandish Art and Material Culture in Asia* (Amsterdam, 2015), 129–40.

[4] J. de Loos-Haaxmann, *De landsverzameling schilderijen in Batavia. Landvoogdsportretten en Compagnieschilders* (Leiden, 1941), 151–52. For Formosa see also K. Zandvliet, "Art and Cartography in the VOC Governor's House in Taiwan," in *Mappae antiquae: liber amicorum Günter Schilder*, ed. P. van Gestel-van het Schip and P. van der Krogt (t'Goy-Mouten, 2007), 579–94.

of these were auctioned together with his estate after his death in 1627. The paintings are specified as follows:

1 small rectangular painting	11 reals of eight
2 landscapes with ebony frame	26 ½
2 rectangular paintings	12 ½
2 Chinese paintings	9
1 big rectangular painting	5
1 ditto smaller	10
2 landscapes framed	10
1 ditto [landscape] without frame	26 ½
1 big ditto [landscape] without frame	25
1 ditto [landscape]	41
1 ditto [landscape] smaller	12 ½
1 ditto [landscape] a bit bigger	14
1 ditto [landscape] framed	16
1 ditto [landscape] framed	12
2 Chinese paintings	7
1 big Dutch painting framed	30 ½
1 ditto	10
3 Chinese paintings on paper	3 ¼
2 small paintings in ebony frame	17 ½
1 big painting, most of it damaged	6.[5]

This manifestly cross-cultural collection was the result of intensified market relations between Western Europe and Southeast Asia as well as Japan and China. That is why, collections in Jakarta and also in Cape Town contained Dutch landscapes, Chinese paintings on paper and Japanese lacquer objects of art.[6]

At the end of the seventeenth and across the eighteenth century, the number of bequeathed estates rose considerably. Numerous paintings are

---

[5] National Archief Den Haag, NA 1.04.02, 1093. Partly published by A. M. Lubberhuizen-van Gelder, "Een oude indische inventaris," in *Cultureel Indië* 8 (1946), 211–20.

[6] M. North, "Art Dealing as Medium of Cultural Transfer," in *Crossing Cultures: Conflict, Migration and Convergence*, held at the University of Melbourne in January 2008 (Melbourne, 2009), 1027–32. For the material VOC World see: *Contingent Lives. Social Identity and Material Culture in the VOC World*, ed. N. Worden (Rondebosch, 2007), see also M. North, "Production and Reception of Art Through European Company Channels in Asia," in *Artistic and Cultural Exchanges Between Europe and Asia, 1400–1900*, ed. M. North (Farnham, 2010), 89–108, here pp. 92–96.

recorded, although they were often specified only with respect to the size or the quality of the frame, as in the case of the officer and member of the Indian Council, Isaac de l'Ostal de Saint-Martin. In his testament of 1695, Governor General Johannes Camphuys bequeathed numerous portraits to his friends and relatives in Batavia, and four volumes containing Chinese, Japanese and "Moorish" (Southeast Asian) drawings were passed on to Pieter van Dam, historian and syndicus of the VOC in Amsterdam.[7]

All subjects known in the Dutch Republic, such as allegories, classical and religious histories, landscapes, still lifes, genre paintings and above all portraits were represented in the households of the upper VOC personnel. Unfortunately, we cannot quantify the relative proportion of the different subjects in the collection, and therefore we cannot yet definitively reconstruct a secularisation of taste as was the case in the Northern Netherlands; for sure, however, landscapes assumed an important role in the collection of the aforementioned Gillis Vinant. During the eighteenth century, pictures became were widely seen in Dutch households in Batavia, although concrete evidence still remains scarce. In 1780, the burgher Johannes Nicolaas Cestbier left behind seven *schilderijtjes* and 34 *schilderijen*, six of which were evidently on glass ("ses schilderijen op glas") (Schepenbank 742). Even in the modest household of Salomon Pieters and Johann Elisabeth Piot (1792), 22 inexpensive paintings and a portrait are registered.[8]

Dutchmen, who often cohabitated with their Eurasian wives or concubines, created a kind of Asian "Dutchness" in their households by merging European and Asian lifestyles and displaying a cross-cultural selection of artefacts in their home.

CHINESE AND MUSLIM HOUSEHOLDS

Other groups comprising Batavian society offer a contrast to the Europeans and Eurasians in terms of art ownership. It would appear that the majority of Chinese households did not display paintings.

---

[7] J. de Loos-Haaxmann, *De landsverzameling schilderijen in Batavia. Landvoogdsportretten en Compagnieschilders* (Leiden, 1941), 152 ff.

[8] Arsip Nasional Republic of Indonesia: Schepenbank 749, see also M. North, "Art and Material Culture in the Cape Colony and Batavia in the Seventeenth and Eighteenth Centuries," in *Mediating Netherlandish Art and Material Culture in Asia*, ed. T. DaCosta Kaufmann and M. North (Amsterdam, 2015), 111–28.

One reason may very well have been the comparatively modest means of the deceased Chinese persons and their household. The process of embellishing and decorating a Chinese home followed certain patterns. Among the first objects acquired for the household were the bird cage, followed by lanterns, copper lamps, mirrors and clocks. Only after these objects were featured in a household, then the Chinese proceeded to acquire decorative paintings and prints, but judging by the taxes levied on the bequeathed estates, it would appear however that these prints and paintings were generally of a modest value. Certainly, it was not that the Chinese could not necessarily afford collectable objects, but they preferred to store their wealth not in artefacts, but in manpower (i.e. slaves and indentured labourers). In addition, households that had no paintings may have instead featured expensive furniture, such as lavishly decorated (Chinese) beds, *dernier cri* gueridons, mirrors and clocks. Certain conditions of fashion and taste, and a certain urge for refinement had to be met before the master of a household or his spouse would decorate the interior walls with objects of art.

Although many Chinese were inclined to splurge on themselves (e.g. clothing, grooming) before buying and collecting art, mention is still made of paintings together with other decorative objects in Chinese households. Some are expressly categorised as Chinese paintings, but most are listed simply as *schilderijen*. A few examples will suffice to provide a general impression (Tables 1 and 2).

Paintings of Chinese and Western origin gained increasing significance in Chinese households where they were displayed together with expensive birdcages, mirrors, clocks and lamps.[9] They reflect thus an intensified cultural exchange between different ethnic groups and households. This is further confirmed by a glance at Muslim households. Especially interesting are the paintings in the estates of members of other ethnic groups.

Although Muslim men and women tended to splurge on personal effects and grooming, including especially lavish clothing and jewellery, they increasingly also came to decorate their households with fashionable East-Asian (Chinese) and Western objects. This, however,

---

[9]This is a very different situation than in the Cape, where the modest household of a Chinese woman named Thisgingno, who had no wall decoration apart from curtains, can be regarded as typical; J. C. Armstrong, "The Estate of a Chinese Woman in the Mid-Eighteenth Century at the Cape of Good Hope," in *Contingent Lives: Social Identity and Material Culture in the VOC World*, ed. N. Worden (Cape Town, 2007), 75–90.

Table 1 Sample of Chinese inventories in Batavia with works of art (Compiled by the Author)

Year	Deceased person	Art objects owned	Hammer price	Arsip Nasional
1779	Be Loeykong, Chinese captain of Ambon	1 painting	0.3 Rd.	Schepenbank 635
1783	Tjoa Tjienthouw	1 Chinese cage 1 pendulum clock	27 Rd. 11.2 Rd.	Schepenbank 743
1789	Nie Bokseeng	A bunch of Chinese paintings		Boedelkamer 63
1789	Tje Tjoenko	2 porcelain elephants 1 copper lanthern and 3 Chinese paintings 1 guilded cage and 3 paintings 7 Chinese paintings		Boedelkamer 63
1790	Thee Imkon	A big Chinese painting 2 oval mirrors with guilded frames		Schepenbank 751
1790	Tan Zinko	1 Frisian clock (a *friese Klok*) 2 mirrors 2 oval mirrors		Schepenbank 751
1790	Vrouw Oey Tjoenko	1 Chinese painting on glass 1 Chinese painted and guilded shelf (*rak*)	6 Rd.	Boedelkamer 82
1791	Njo Samtijauw, living close to the *Crocolse* bridge	2 paintings in golden frames		
1791	Lim Hantan, bankrupt	5 bunches of paintings (5 *ps. [partijs] schildereyen*) 3 small mirrors 2 mirrors	3.36 Rd. 16 Rd. 48 Rd.	Schepenbank 748
1794	Tan Koeko	One mirror and two paintings beside his rich holdings of textiles 1 table clock		Schepenbank 755
1795	Lauw Tamtjong	2 bunches of Chinese paintings	4.36 Rd.	Schepenbank 757

(continued)

DOMESTIC INTERIORS IN SEVENTEENTH- AND EIGHTEENTH-CENTURY BATAVIA   111

Table 1 (continued)

Year	Deceased person	Art objects owned	Hammer price	Arsip Nasional
1796	Tan Tjoeyseeng	2 mirrors 2 small mirrors 1 copper hanging lamp		Schepenbank 758
1796	Tan Soeyko	1 shelf, 2 small mirros and 3 chinese paintings (*1 rak, 2 spiegeltjes en drie Chines Schilderyen*) 2 mirrors 1 Frisian clock	9 Rd. 36 20 Rd. 24 Rd.	Schepenbank 758
1796	Lim Konghiem	One Chinese painting 4 paintings on glass 6 paintings are listed and were sold together with other goods 1 Frisian clock	9.24 Rd. 13 Rd.	Schepenbank 759
1800	Tjoa Tjouwko	2 mirrors 1 mirror and 3 paintings 1 chandelier (*een glase kroon*) 1 copper hanging lamp	11.24 Rd. 12.24 Rd. 27 Rd. 36 Rd.	Schepenbank 761
1804	Tjan Tjeengko	9 paintings 24 paintings 23 paintings 2 mirrors 1 Frisian clock	37 Rd. 58 Rd. 43 Rd. 39 Rd. 67 Rd.	Schepenbank 762
1805	Tan Teengko	A bunch (*partby*) of paintings, worth more than his Chinese books and maps	22 Rd.	Schepenbank 744
1812	Vrouw Giam Hongnio	8 damaged paintings		Boedelkamer 80
1812	Lie Djoeseeng	11 paintings	20 Rd.	Boedelkamer 80
1813	Lie Leenio (Chinese widow of a Dutchman)	2 Chinese lantherns 3 paintings	25 Rd.	Boedelkamer 67

Arsip Nasional, Schepenbank and Boedelkamer

Table 2 Sample of Batavia inventories of non-Dutch, non-Chinese inhabitants (Compiled by the Author)

Year	Deceased person	Art objects owned	Hammer price	Arsip Nasional
1788	Free Buginese woman Saliera	4 mirrors and 2 candlesticks (*blakkers*) 2 copper lamps		
1789	Moor Bamba Sa Assan Miera left behind	5 paintings, pendulum clock (*a stand boorlogie*) a guilded cage		Boedelkamer 64
1790	Arab *vrouw* Sariepa Aloeya Binli Achmat Aboeff Tayheep	2 Chinese cages 3 white copper hanging lamps	65 Rd. 45 Rd.	Boedelkamer 64
1790	Free Macassar Abdul Ilalik, when he died in 1790	Building materials, mirrors 4 paintings 1 frisian clock (*friese Klok*)		Boedelkamer 64
1790	Abdul Cadier Balinese Captain (*from Macassar*)	1 double Chinese cage 2 candle sticks 1 copper hanging lanthern 3 mirrors with guilded frames 2 big and 2 small mirrors A part from rich clothing and modest jewelry		Boedelkamer 64
1791	Insolvent *overledene Moor* Bappoe Ibrahim Poele	6 paintings in a decorative golden frame 3 mirrors 1 Chinese cage 2 candlesticks A silver pocket watch		Schepenbank 749
1794	Moor Smaon Oesien Bandarie	1 painting		Boedelkamer 152

(continued)

Table 2 (continued)

Year	Deceased person	Art objects owned	Hammer price	Arsip Nasional
[Year?]	Mochamad Miera Sase	One small round Dutch table (*kleyne ronde nederlandse tafel*)	3 Rd.	Boedelkamer 152
		one big painting, 13 prints, 2 broken mirrors and 4 broken candlesticks (*blakkers*)	6.24 Rd.	
		3 copper hanging lamps	50 Rd.	
		3 English copper lantherns	90 Rd.	
		A part from expensive jewelry		
1804	Balinese Captain Abdul Kadier Babandam	3 lantherns	35 Rd.	Schepenbank 764
		3 mirrors	15 Rd.	
		A golden pocket watch	20 Rd.	
1811	Free Balinese vrouw Asamie	A part from rich jewelry	40 Rd.	Boedelkamer?
		A copper hanging lamp	350 Rd.	
		4 vitrines	18 Rd.	
		4 damaged paintings		
1813	Free Balinese Kaliep Oemar	Wooden candlesticks (*blakkers*)		Boedelkamer 67
		3 paintings and a handing case with indigedions books (*bang kastje met inlandsche boeken*)		

Arsip Nasional, Schepenbank and Boedelkamer

requires further investigation by differentiating between the various ethnic groups. Most of the Malays and Balinese did not leave any traces in the archives, and as result we nearly know anything about their domestic interiors.

Cultural (Secondary) Markets

Estate auctions played a significant role in facilitating the interaction of the different ethnic groups and their respective (material) cultural markets. Although the few existing auction protocols of the seventeenth century lead us to assume that it was above all Dutch burghers who purchased paintings, furniture and even Asian objects from the estates of their fellow citizens, by the eighteenth-century auctions had clearly become a cultural touchpoint and an art forum for all ethnic groups. A curious example arises from the auction protocol of the late and bankrupt Armenian merchant Cosorop Petrus, whose belongings were sold off in November 1798.[10] In addition to a large stock of Madeira wine, this rich household was brought under the hammer with Dutch, Chinese and Muslim bidders purchasing different objects. One Chinese named as Sim Tjimko appears to have had an eye for decorative objects. First of all, he purchased a large painting (*Een grote schilderij*) for the price of 17 Rd. The size and the price let us suppose that this was a large Dutch painting that found its way from an Armenian household into a Chinese household and perhaps even further if Sim Tjimko acted as an agent, or proxy, for yet another client. He also acquired three hanging lamps made of copper for a total of 27 Rd, four copper spittoons for 22 Rd and an ensemble of day beds (*rustbanken*), wicker chairs and other chairs, gueridons and two gambling tables for a total of 94 Rd. Apart from several bottles of wine, Piro Mochamat (who might be a Muslim or possibly even a Christian Mardijker, according to his first name Piro = Pero) purchased an expensive copper lantern and a precious table clock encased in glass for 74 Rd.

Unfortunately, we know very little about the successful bidders on this and other estate sales. Most of the buyers seem to have been in the business of purchasing in any case, as merchants or small traders. Others probably tried to obtain some decorative objects for their homes.

---

[10] Arsip Nasional, Schepenbank 1718 (1798).

Whether family connections (as documented in other estate sales)[11] played a role, is not always evident or conclusive.

REPRESENTATION OF THE VOC IN ASIA

Art, however, was not only present in private households and circulated via estate auctions. To create legitimacy the Dutch East India Company commissioned portraits of the Governors General. These portraits form—as artistic testimony of the Dutch presence in Asia—a special corpus of paintings that has for a long time dominated our view on Dutch colonial painting. This gallery of portraits, "*de oude landvoogdsportretten*" represented continuity and thereby legitimacy of Dutch power in Southeast Asia. They are influenced by the tradition of European princely portraits, especially the portrait galleries of European dynasties. Accordingly, the VOC gave portraits of the Dutch Republican "surrogate dynasty", the House of Orange, as presents to Asian rulers.[12] Furthermore, it stimulated to a considerable, but varying extend also the presence of art in colonial households.

The model for the gallery of portraits in Batavia was the still-extant gallery of the Portuguese viceroys of Goa, which had been visited and admired by Dutch visitors on their way to the east. The origins of the portrait gallery date back into the mid-seventeenth century, when the VOC commissioned a series of ten portraits that could been have painted by Philips Angel. Later, it became common for a Governor General at the end of his period of service to commission a portrait of himself. The majority of the portraits was painted in Asia, although in the eighteenth-century portraits of the Governor Generals were increasingly painted in the Netherlands. The representational quality of the individual portrait compared with the portraits of the predecessor was a major issue of the portrait commission. However, the portrait of Governor General in the assembly hall of the VOC in Batavia constituted only one of several family portraits. For example, Rijcklof van Goens, who established

---

[11] T. Randle, "Patterns of Consumption at Auctions: A Case Study of Three Estates," in *Contingent Lives. Social Identity and Material Culture in the VOC World*, ed. N. Worden (Cape Town, 2007), 53–74.

[12] O. Mörke, *"Stadtholder" oder "Staetholder"?: Die Funktion des Hauses Oranien und seines Hofes in der politischen Kultur der Republik der Vereinigten Niederlande im 17. Jahrhundert* (Münster and Hamburg, 1997).

the Dutch power in Ceylon and the Malabar coast, commissioned in the mid-seventeenth century several portraits and other subjects from Luttichuys, van der Helst, Govert Flinck and the van de Velde painter family "tot de voyagie nae India" (for the voyage to India). Some of the portraits remained as memoria in Holland, other paintings were shipped for representative purposes to Asia.[13]

In the eighteenth century, it became common for Governors General to have themselves depicted holding the staff of office and richly decorated coat of arms. Moreover, it seemed most fashionable to commission a portrait by a prominent painter in Holland. The East Frisian Governor General sat for a portrait from Philipp van Dijk in The Hague, and commissioned another by J. M. Quinkhard. He took both portraits to Asia, where a copy integrating elements of both was made. The final stage of aesthetic transfer from Europe to Asia occurred with the portrait of Willem Arnold Alting by Johann Friedrich August Tischbein. The German court painter Tischbein seems to have finished the portrait in the Netherlands, using perhaps an already existing portrait. The salon piece of 1788 depicts Alting, a corrupt and greedy Governor General in the declining years of the VOC, as an elegant French-style representative of the Ancien Regime.[14]

Interestingly, it was not only the portraits of governors that decorated the council room of the government at Batavia Fort. Contemporary images, such as the image from Johann Wolfgang Heydt's 1744 travel account from the East Indies show not only a big umbrella (parasol) under which the councillors gathered. Moreover, the entrance of the

---

[13] E. Schmitt, et al. (ed.), *Kaufleute als Kolonialherren. Die Handelswelt der Niederländer vom Kap der Guten Hoffnung bis Nagasaki 1600–1800* (Bamberg, 1988), 121–22; Hugo K's Jacob, "Father and Son van Goens in Action: War and Diplomacy in the Relations Between the Malabar Rulers and the Dutch East India Company 1658–1682," in *Maritime Malabar and the Europeans 1500–1962*, ed. Kuzhippallil Skaria Mathew (Kolkata, 2003), 313–28.

[14] H. Seemann, *Spuren einer Freundschaft. Deutsch-Indonesische Beziehungen vom 16. bis 19. Jahrhundert* (Jakarta, 2000), 45–49; Roelof van Gelder, *Het Oost-Indisch avontuur: Duitsers in dienst van de VOC (1600–1800)* (Nijmegen, 1997), 185–87; F. S. Gaastra, *De geschiedenis van de VOC* (Zutphen, 2002), 166–70; D. van Duuren, "Governors-General and Civilians. Portrait Art in the Dutch East Indies from the Seventeenth to the Nineteenth Century," in *Pictures from the Tropics. Paintings by Western Artists During the Dutch Colonial Period in Indonesia*, ed. M.-O. Scalliet, K. van Brakel, D. van Duuren, and J. ten Kate (Wijk en Aalburg, 1999), 90–102, here pp. 95–97.

chamber was decorated by a Chinese teak screen, which documents the cross-cultural decoration of the VOC council chamber.[15]

After the re-establishment of Dutch power in Indonesia in 1815, the Gallery of Governors General was continued, and indigenous painters, as the Javanese painter of landscapes, Raden Saleh, took part in the production.[16] The portrait gallery came to an end during decolonisation after the Second World War II, when the portraits were removed and sent back to the Netherlands.

The governor portraits, however, also influenced portraits of indigenous rulers, such as Sayfoedin, Sultan of Tidore. Together with the Sultan of Ternate, Sayfoedin had been pressed by the VOC to sign an exclusive supply contract that was supposed to ensure a Dutch monopoly in cloves and nutmeg. In 1667, the Sultan of Tidore, whose power in the Moluccas was supported by the Dutch, served as their ally in the campaign against Macassar (1667). Probably in this context, Sayfoedin's portrait was painted and handed over in exchange for a portrait of his ally, the Dutch commander in the Macassar campaign Cornelis Speelmans. The portrait made its way to Holland and via the Amsterdam art market into the collection of the Polish noble family Czartoryski in Pulawy. There Sayfoedin's portrait was integrated into a gallery of heroes struggling for freedom (together with paintings of William Tell, Joan of Arc, George Washington, Tipu Sultan, etc.).[17]

Conclusion

This chapter has traced the emergence of a domestic material culture across ethnicities and cultures in seventeenth- and eighteenth-century Batavia. When people moved to Batavia from Europe or East Asia,

---

[15] D. Odell, "Public Identity and Material Culture in Dutch Batavia," in *Crossing Cultures: Conflict, Migration and Convergence: The Proceedings of the 32nd International Congress in the History of Art*, ed. J. Anderson (Comité International d'Histoire de l'Art, CIHA). The University of Melbourne, 13–18 January 2008 (Carlton, VIC, 2009), 253–57, here p. 255.

[16] Ibid., 98–100.

[17] M. North, "Koloniale Kunstwelten in Ostindien. Kulturelle Kommunikation im Umkreis der Handelskompanien," in *Jahrbuch für Europäische Überseegeschichte* 5 (2005): 55–72, here p. 65; K. Zandvliet (ed.), *De Nederlandse ontmoeting met Azië 1600–1950* (Zwolle, 2002), 120–22; and National museum Krakow, Collection Czartoryski (Warsaw, 1978), 6–21.

they brought with them only a small number of art objects for essentially decorative or commemorative purposes. If they wanted more art and decorative elements in their homes or wished to climb the social ladder through a conspicuous display of wealth, they had to commission art objects or buy them on the open market. An important market instrument for second-hand goods was provided by estate auctions. Thus the exchange assumed many forms and directions. On the one hand, "Dutch" decoration patterns were disseminated via the VOC and the upper social strata of the Company to the middle classes and the different indigenous groups. On the other hand, Chinese styles of decoration were received by Europeans in Batavia, who bought and displayed Chinese (and of course also Japanese) cultural goods of many kinds. Different identities emerged, although today we still know very little about the motives and the role that material objects played in constructing or reinforcing these identities. More evidence and research is required, in analysing the different mediating roles of the VOC, the Europeans and its/their host societies in Asia.[18] Furthermore, future research should examine the global aspects of material culture. There is a growing pool of evidence that the eighteenth century saw the gradual formation of a global material culture. Domestic interiors of the elites and upper middle classes across Europe, Asia and North America seem to be affected by remarkably similar fashions.[19] If this hypothesis can be sustained and validated, a crucial follow-up question would necessarily be how such trends and fashions were communicated, transmitted and received across continents, countries and cultures.

[18] T. DaCosta Kaufmann and M. North, Mediating Cultures, in *Mediating Netherlandish Art and Material Culture in Asia*, ed. T. DaCosta Kaufmann and M. North (Amsterdam, 2015), 9–24.

[19] See, for example, D. Goodmann, and K. Norberg (eds.), *Furnishing the Eighteenth Century: What Furniture Can Tell Us About the European and American Past* (New York, 2007); A. Vickery, *Behind Closed Doors. At Home in Georgian England* (London, New Haven, 2009); and T. H. Breen, *The Marketplace of Revolution: How Consumer Politics Shaped American Independence* (New York, 2004), an early example of the materially connected Atlantic and Indian Ocean worlds provides the catalog D. L. Krohn and Peter N. Miller (eds.), *Dutch New York Between East and West. The World of Margrieta Van Varick* (New York, 2010). See also M. North, "Towards a Global Material Culture. Domestic Interiors in the Atlantic and Other Worlds," in *Cultural Exchange and Consumption Patterns in the Age of Enlightenment*, ed. V. Hyden-Hanscho, R. Pieper, and W. Stangl. The Eighteenth Century and the Habsburg Monarchy International Series, Vol. 6 (Bochum 2013), 81–96.

Bibliography

Armstrong, James C. 2007. The Estate of a Chinese Woman in the Mid-Eighteenth Century at the Cape of Good Hope. In *Contingent Lives: Social Identity and Material Culture in the VOC World*, ed. Nigel Worden, 75–90. Cape Town: Rondebosch.
Bosma, Ulbe, and Remco Raben. 2008. *Being "Dutch" in the Indies: A History of Creolisation and Empire, 1500–1920*. Singapore: NUS Press.
Breen, T.H. 2004. *The Marketplace of Revolution: How Consumer Politics Shaped American Independence*. New York: Oxford University Press.
de Loos-Haaxmann, Jeanne. 1941. *De landsverzameling schilderijen in Batavia. Landvoogdsportretten en Compagnieschilders*. Leiden: A.W. Sijthoff's Uitgeversmaatschappij.
Gaastra, Femme S. 2002. *De geschiedenis van de VOC*. Zutphen: Walburg Pers.
Gellman Taylor, Jean. 2009. *The Social World of Batavia: Europeans and Eurasians in Colonial Indonesia*. New Perspectives in SE Asian Studies. Madison: The University of Wisconsin Press.
Goodmann, Dena, and Kathryn Norberg (eds.). 2007. *Furnishing the Eighteenth Century: What Furniture Can Tell Us About the European and American Past*. New York: Routledge.
Jacob, Hugo K's. 2003. Father and Son van Goens in Action: War and Diplomacy in the Relations Between the Malabar Rulers and the Dutch East India Company 1658–1682. In *Maritime Malabar and the Europeans 1500–1962*, ed. Kuzhippallil Skaria Mathew, 313–328. Kolkata: Hope India Publications.
Kaufmann, Thomas DaCosta, and Michael North. 2015. Mediating Cultures. In *Mediating Netherlandish Art and Material Culture in Asia*, ed. Thomas DaCosta Kaufmann and Michael North, 9–24. Amsterdam Studies in the Golden Age. Amsterdam: Amsterdam University Press.
Krohn, Deborah L., and Peter N. Miller (eds.). 2010. *Dutch New York Between East and West. The World of Margrieta Van Varick*. New York: Yale University Press.
Lubberhuizen-van Gelder, A.M. 1946. Een oude indische inventaris. *Cultureel Indië* 8: 211–220.
Mörke, Olaf. 1997. *"Stadtholder" oder "Staetholder"? Die Funktion des Hauses Oranien und seines Hofes in der politischen Kultur der Republik der Vereinigten Niederlande im 17. Jahrhundert*. Münster and Hamburg: LIT.
Nas, Peter J.M. 2015. 'Indische' Architecture in Indonesia. In *Mediating Netherlandish Art and Material Culture in Asia*, ed. Thomas DaCosta Kaufmann and Michael North. Amsterdam: Amsterdam University Press.
Niemeijer, E.H. 1996. *Calvinisme en koloniale stadscultuur, Batavia 1619–1725*. Amsterdam: Vrije Universiteit te Amsterdam.

North, Michael. 2005. Koloniale Kunstwelten in Ostindien. Kulturelle Kommunikation im Umkreis der Handelskompanien. *Jahrbuch für Europäische Überseegeschichte* 5: 55–72.

North, Michael. 2009. Art Dealing as Medium of Cultural Transfer. In *Crossing Cultures: Conflict, Migration and Convergence*, 1027–1032. Melbourne: University of Melbourne (January 2008).

North, Michael. 2010. Production and Reception of Art Through European Company Channels in Asia. In *Artistic and Cultural Exchanges Between Europe and Asia, 1400–1900*, ed. Michael North, 89–108. Farnham: Ashgate.

North, Michael. 2013. Towards a Global Material Culture. Domestic Interiors in the Atlantic and Other Worlds. In *Cultural Exchange and Consumption Patterns in the Age of Enlightenment*, vol. 6, ed. V. Hyden-Hanscho, R. Pieper, and W. Stangl, 81–96. The Eighteenth Century and the Habsburg Monarchy International Series. Bochum 2013.

North, Michael. 2015. Art and Material Culture in the Cape Colony and Batavia in the Seventeenth and Eighteenth Centuries. In *Mediating Netherlandish Art and Material Culture in Asia*, ed. Thomas DaCosta Kaufmann and Michael North, 111–128. Amsterdam: Amsterdam University Press.

Odell, Dawn. 2009. Public Identity and Material Culture in Dutch Batavia. In *Crossing Cultures: Conflict, Migration and Convergence. The Proceedings of the 32th International Congress in the History of Art*, ed. J. Anderson, 253–257. Comité International d'Histoire de l'Art (CIHA). Carlton, VIC: Miegunyah Press, The University of Melbourne (13–18 January 2008).

Randle, Tracey. 2010. Patterns of Consumption at Auctions: A Case Study of Three Estates. In *Contingent Lives. Social Identity and Material Culture in the VOC World*, ed. Nigel Worden, 53–74. Basingstoke, Hampshire [u.a.]: Palgrave Macmillan.

Schmitt, Eberhard, et al. (eds.). 1988. *Kaufleute als Kolonialherren. Die Handelswelt der Niederländer vom Kap der Guten Hoffnung bis Nagasaki 1600–1800*. Bamberg: Buchners.

Seemann, Heinrich. 2000. *Spuren einer Freundschaft. Deutsch-Indonesische Beziehungen vom 16. bis 19. Jahrhundert*. Jakarta: Cipta Loka Caraka.

van Duuren, David. 1999. Governors-General and Civilians. Portrait Art in the Dutch East Indies from the Seventeenth to the Nineteenth Century. In *Pictures from the Tropics. Paintings by Western Artists During the Dutch Colonial Period in Indonesia*, ed. Marie-Odette Scalliet, Koos van Brakel, David van Duuren, and Jeannette ten Kate, 90–102. Wijk en Aalburg: Koninklijk Instituut voor de Tropen.

van Gelder, Roelof. 1997. *Het Oost-Indisch avontuur: Duitsers in dienst van de VOC (1600–1800)*. Nijmegen: SON.

Vickery, Amanda. 2009. *Behind Closed Doors. At Home in Georgian England*. London, New Haven: Yale University Press.

Worden, Nigel (ed.). 2007. *Contingent Lives. Social Identity and Material Culture in the VOC World*. Cape Town: Rondebosch.

Zandvliet, Kees. 2007. Art and Cartography in the VOC Governor's House in Taiwan. In *Mappae antiquae: liber amicorum Günter Schilder*, ed. Paula van Gestel-van het Schip and Peter van der Krogt, 579–594. t'Goy-Mouten: Hes & De Graaf.

INDEX

A
Abaca, 51, 53
'*Abangan*' (the red group), 96
Acapulco, 3, 6, 33, 48–50
Aceh, 48, 84
Achuete/atsuete, 50
Act of National Culture (1942), 81
Addictiveness, 79
Africa, 3, 4, 7, 15, 16, 33, 49, 85
Aguacate, 51
Aklan, 51
Alcalde mayores, 58
Alcina, Ignacio, 66
Alcohol, 87, 92, 94–96
Alcoholic beverages, 76
Aldermen's court/*schepenbank*, 105
Alhajas, 60
Alkaloids, 76, 77, 84, 86, 87, 91, 92
Al-Qadri ruling, 94
American gum, 82
Americans, 6, 9, 34, 48, 67, 91
Americas, 6, 11, 14–21, 25, 33–35, 44, 45, 49, 58, 82, 83
Andaya, Barbara, 58, 59
Angadanan Viejo, 46

Angel, Philips, 115
Animism, 93
Annatto (*Bixa orellana*), 50
Antipolo, 55
Arabica coffee, 12, 90
Areca nut (Areca catechu), 50, 76–79, 81, 82, 84
Areca palm, 77, 78, 81, 82
Arecoline, 76
Arquitectura Espanola en Filipinas (1565–1800), 66
Arquitectura mestiza, 66
Art collections, 106
Asia, 4, 6, 10–17, 21, 23, 27–30, 49, 76, 93, 104, 106–108, 115–118
Asian, 5, 6, 10, 14, 16, 20, 21, 25, 26, 28, 31, 34, 36, 37, 103, 104, 106, 108, 114, 115
Asian Dutchness, 108
Assam tea, 89
Augustinians, 4, 5, 9, 45, 48, 52, 54, 62, 65, 70
Augustinians (from 1565 onwards), 54
Ayudhya, 78

B

Bailey, Gauvin Alexander, 4, 9, 67
Bajo la Campana, 54
Balambangan, 95
Balinese, 57, 104, 112–114
Balon Santa Lucia, 56
Bamboo, 60
Banana leaves, 64, 84
Bananas, 83
Bandanese, 104
Bangkok, 82, 85
Banten, 94
Baro, 51
Baroque-Romanesque style, 62
Baroquization of Philippine religious architecture, 67
Batangas, 54, 55
Batavia, 10, 11, 21, 25, 26, 35, 36, 95, 104–106, 108, 110, 112, 115–118
Batavian society, 104, 108
Bengal, 30, 31, 104
Bernal, Rafael, 50, 51
Betel chewing, 76–82, 84–86, 89, 95, 96
Betel leaf (Piper betel), 50, 77, 81, 82
Betel (*sirih*), 11, 30, 32, 50, 60, 76–89, 92, 94–96
Betel vine, 77, 82
Biblioteca Nacional de España in Madrid, 65
Bicol, 57
Binondo, 4, 54
Biombo/byobu, 17, 33, 34
Bird cages, 109
Black tea, 89
Borneo, 48
Borobudor, ninth-century Buddhist stupa of, 68
Buddhist monks, 92, 95
Bulacan, 55
Burma, 7, 21, 25, 30, 31, 79, 83, 85, 91
Buyobuyo, 50

C

Caffeine, 76, 78
Cagayan style, 46
Cagayan Valley, 46
California coast, 48
Cambodia, 3, 7, 21, 23, 25, 82, 86, 93
Camellia sinensis, 78
Camisa, 51
Camphuys, Johannes, 108
Cannabis, 76
Cape Town, 107, 109, 115
Capiz, 65
Catholic, 3–5, 12, 18, 50, 53, 59, 93
Caveat, 82
Cavite, 55
Cebu, 48
Ceylon Directory, 90
Cham, 93
'Cheroots', 83, 85, 86
Chilli peppers, 50
China/Chinese, 1, 3–5, 8–12, 14, 16, 20, 22, 28, 30, 33–37, 45, 48–53, 55, 60, 67, 78, 81, 83, 87–89, 92, 104–112, 114, 117, 118
Chinese artisans, 3, 16, 53, 67
Chinese households, 108, 109
Chinese mythology, 68
Chocolate (cocoa), 12, 76, 87, 92, 93, 95
Chocolate (*Theobroma cacao*), 12, 50, 76, 87, 91–93, 95
Christ Child, 3, 62, 65
Christians, 3, 18, 34, 54, 60, 66, 104, 114

Church-fortress, 62
Churrigueresque style, 61
Cigarettes, 11, 83–87, 96
Cigars, 82, 84, 85
Civility, 82, 89
Clarence-Smith, William G., 11, 12, 50, 76, 90–93
Coconuts, 50, 60, 64, 66
Coen, Jan Pietersz, 104
Coffee, 12, 76, 87, 90–94
Coffee rust (*Hemileia vastatrix*), 90
Common Era, 87
Confucian, 92
Conquest, 55, 69
Contrafuertes, 59
Conventos, 57
Coromandel, 30
Coseteng, Alicia, 66, 69
Cotton, 53, 60
Crawfurd, John, 83
Cushner, Nicholas, 58

D
Dagregisters, 25
Daoist, 92
Daraga, 57
Daraga church, 67
Dar al-Islam, 93
Darul Islam guerillas, 95
Dean, Carolyn, 68
Decolonisation, 117
De Houtmans, Cornelius, 104
De la Loubère, Simon, 89, 92, 95
Dernier cri gueridons, 109
De Urdaneta, Andrés, 9, 48
Diaz-Trechuelo, Maria Lourdes, 3, 44, 66
Dipterocárpus, 24
Disease, 14, 79, 88
Dominican order, 46

Dominicans, 4, 46, 54
Don Bartolome Palatino from Paete, 55
Dupax, 46
Dutch, 9–11, 23–28, 31, 32, 34–36, 78, 79, 84, 85, 89, 91, 104–108, 114–118
Dutch East India Company (VOC), 6, 7, 9, 10, 12, 15, 18, 25, 28, 30, 32, 90, 104–109, 115, 116, 118
Dutch house owners, 106
Dutch Republic, 105, 108

E
Earthquake Baroque, 47
East Africa, 77
Ecclesiastical Cabildo of Manila, 59
Elena Estrada de Gerlero, 65
Elites, 5, 11, 50, 51, 79, 83, 84, 90, 91, 118
El Salvador, 50
Encomendero, 59
Encomiendas, 58
English East-India Company, 104
Entrepôts in Asia, 49
Epigraphic data, 77
Estate auctions, 114, 115, 118
Estate chamber/boedelkamer, 105, 110–112
Ethiopia, 12, 90
Eurasia, 104
Eurasian, 104, 105, 108

F
Façades, 9, 43–46, 55, 61, 65
Fermented tea, 79
Field-Marshal Phibunsongkhram, 81
Filipino Baroque, 44
Filipino elements, 44

Filipino-ness, 46
Filipino Rococo, 44
Filipino style, 9, 48, 67, 69
Flying buttresses, 46
Foreign elements, 45
Forts, 60, 64
Franciscans, 5, 18, 54, 55, 57
Frank, Andre Gunder, 14
Fray Manuel Murguia, 52
Free Asian, 104, 105
Freeburghers, 104
French conquest, 88
Fujian, 50
Funerals, 86

G

Galleon trade, 3, 7, 8, 33, 47–49, 59
Gallery of portraits, 115
'*Gambir*' (cutch), 84, 85
Gender issue, 76
Germ theory, 79
Global history, 6–8, 14–16
Gluta lacifera, 23
Gluta usitata, 22, 24
Goa, 4, 7, 26, 27, 31, 33, 115
Gold, 17, 21, 22, 28, 48, 60, 68
Gold working, 68
Gothic and Romanesque aspects, 62
Governor-General, 106, 108
Green tea, 87–89, 92, 93
Guatemala, 50
Guava, 44, 61, 62
Guisar, 51

H

Hadhramaut (East Yemen), 94
Hadhrami, 94
Herbicides, 76
Hindu, 94
Hindu-Buddhist, 68

Hispanic gastronomy, 50
Hispano-Dutch War (1621–1648), 58, 60
Hispano-Filipino, 66
Horacio de la Costa, 59
Horses, 44, 49, 50, 61, 64
House of Orange, 106, 115
Hybridity, 68
Hybrid nature, 45, 68
Hygiene, 11, 81, 82

I

Iberians, 4, 7, 8, 11, 17, 26, 36, 82
Ilocano, 45
Ilocano Baroque, 46
Ilocos region, 45
Iloilo, 43, 51, 64, 67, 70
India, 6, 11, 14, 18, 21, 27, 28, 30, 31, 77, 78, 81, 89, 116
Indian Ocean, 6, 36, 77, 105, 118
Indio sculptor, Joséph Bergaño or *Sarhento Itak*, 52
Indoasian, 104
IndoChina, 82, 91
Indonesia, 80, 86, 89–91, 93, 94, 105, 116, 117
Indonesian archipelago, 9, 12, 48, 68, 105
Insecticides, 76
Interior decoration, 105
Intramuros, 55
Isaac de l'Ostal de Saint-Martin, 108
Islam, 45, 56, 93–95
Italian Baroque, 55

J

Jackfruit (*nanca*), 60
Jakarta/Jacatra, 21, 25, 26, 104, 105, 107, 116

Japan, 4, 7, 8, 10, 11, 14, 16–28, 30–36, 45, 107
Java, 10–12, 57, 68, 79, 80, 83–87, 89–91, 96, 104
Java war (1825-1830), 78
Javellana, René, 44, 47, 58
Jesuits, 5, 17, 18, 54, 55, 59
Johann Elisabeth Piot, 108
Johannes Nicolaas Cestbier, 108
Johann Friedrich August Tischbein, 116
Jolo archipelago, 48
Jose, Regalado Trota, 4
Juan de los Santos, 52

K
Kalimantan, 86, 94
Kartasura, 83
Kedu, 84
Kelantan, 86
Kelemen, Pal, 45
'*Klobot*', 11, 83–86
Korea, 16, 22, 31, 92
'*Kretek*', 11, 84, 85
Kunstkammer, 32

L
Lacquer, 6, 7, 16–28, 30–34, 36, 107
Laguna, 51, 52, 55, 57, 59, 61, 67
Laguna de Bay, 54, 55
Latin American, 45, 65, 66
Leche flan, 57
Legarda Jr., Benito, 45, 70
Leibsohn, Dana, 6, 68
Linguistic data, 77
Lisbon, 4, 7, 17–19, 26, 31, 33
Livestock-raising, 60
Love, 68, 78
Low, James, 78, 83, 85
Lumban, 51
Luzon, 8, 44, 45, 47, 48, 50, 51, 55, 67

M
Macassar, 117
Madura, 90
Maestros-de-obras, 62
Magellan, 66
Maghrib, 93
Mainland South East Asia, 12, 83, 88, 93, 95
Maize, 49, 83, 86
Majayjay, 59
Makassarese, 89–91
Malacca, 7, 21, 25, 26, 33, 48
Malaya, 78, 85–87, 89, 91, 94
Malay Peninsula, 48
Malay(s), 48, 80, 83, 84, 86, 104, 114
Malaysia, 80
Malinalco, 65, 66
Maluku, 60, 90
Manila, 1, 3–8, 17, 21, 33–35
Manila galleons, 7, 33, 49, 50
Marcel Proust, 96
Mardijkers, 104, 105, 114
Marikina Valley, 55
Maritime South East Asia, 6, 12, 49, 89
Marriage, 67, 78, 80, 89, 104
Marx, Karl, 14
'*Mascada*', 86
Material culture, 11, 12, 15, 106–109, 115, 117, 118
Maynilad, 48
Melanorrhoea usitata, 23
Mental functions, 76
Mexico, 3, 9, 16, 18, 33, 34, 49, 50, 52, 60, 65
Miag-ao church, 62, 64, 67
Miang, 79
Miguel Lopez de Legazpi, 48
Military coup 1932 (Thailand), 81
Milk, 88, 89
Mindanao, 50, 60
Mochamat, Piro, 114
Modernity, 11, 82

The Moluccas, 9, 48, 104, 117
"Moren", 105
Morocco, 64, 93
Morong, 55, 67
Mother-of-pearl, 21, 22
Mughal, 27, 28, 30, 31
Multicultural, 104
Multiethnic, 104
Murillo Velarde, Pedro, Jesuit Father, 59
Musa textilis, a species of banana, 51, 53
Muslim households, 108
Muslims, 9, 11, 12, 48, 60, 64, 67, 93–96, 104, 109, 114

N
Namrack, 23, 25
Nanban/namban, 17, 18, 26–29, 34
Nanban shikki, 17, 26
National Archives of Indonesia, 105
Newson, Linda, 58, 60
New Spain, 5, 7, 33, 48, 65
New World, 9, 12, 33, 44, 46, 47, 49–51, 54, 60, 61, 65, 69, 91
New World flora and fauna, 9, 44, 47, 61
New World produce, 46
Nicolas de la Cruz Bagay, 60
Nicotine, 76
Nineteenth century, 78, 79, 84, 85, 88, 89, 91, 116
Nutrition, 76
Nyai, 106

O
Old World, 49
Oolong tea, 89, 94
Opiates, 76
Oral cancer, 79

Orphanage/*weeskamer*, 105
Our Lady of Turumba, 57

P
Padris, 94
Paete, 55, 56, 65, 67
Paete church, 55
Paintings, 4, 11, 17, 54, 105–117
Pakil, 55, 56
Paletada, a thin plaster of stucco, 57
Palm, 62, 66, 77, 83, 86
Panay, 51, 60, 64, 67
Pan-ay church, 51, 54
Panocha the brown, unrefined, coarse grained sugar, 51
Pansipit River, 56
Papaya, 44, 51, 60–62, 64
Paradise garden murals, 65
Paraphernalia, 78
Pasig River, 4, 48, 54
Pattani, 48
Pediment, 46, 47, 52, 61, 62, 65
Pekalongan, 84
Penang, 78
Persia, 3, 93
Peterson, Jeanette Favrot, 65
Petrus, Cosorop, 114
Philippines, 3, 4, 8, 11, 12, 34, 45–48, 50, 54, 58, 68–70, 77, 81, 82, 84–86, 91, 93
Piedra buga, 57
Pieters, Salomon, 108
Piña cloth, a light, luxurious, diaphanous material, 51
Pinang (areca), 84
Pineapple, 44, 46, 50–54
Pineapple motifs, 53
Pinecone, 53
Pipe, 83
Plants, 9, 44, 48–51, 60, 68, 69, 76
Polo (forced labor), 58

Ponder, H.W., 80, 85–87, 90, 91
Pontianak, 94, 96
Porcelain, 3, 10, 20, 31, 36, 37, 62, 88, 106, 110
Portuguese, 4, 7, 9, 17, 19, 24, 26–34, 36, 48, 77, 92, 104, 115
Powdered snuff, 82
Pre-colonial figurative art, 68
Prince Dipanagara, 78, 83
Prito, 51
Probate inventories, 11, 105, 106
Prophet, 94, 96
Protestant, 93
Protestantism, 93
Pulpit, 34, 52

R
Rancherias/cattle ranches, 50
Recollects (1606), 54
Reducciones, 54
Reid, Anthony, 76
Religion, 12, 76, 92, 94, 96
Religious groups, 92
Religious rituals, 11, 76
Representations of conversion, 65
Retablos, 4, 52, 54
Rhus vernicifera/verniciflua, 22
Rice, 58, 60, 65, 80, 83, 86
Robusta, 90
Romblon, 65
Rykyuan junks, 14

S
Sacristan mayor, 52
Saleh, Raden, 117
Saliva, 78–81
San Agustin church, 51, 60
Sandalwood, 60
San Joaquin church, 65
San Mateo, 55

San Pablo, 52
San Pedro Makati, 54
Santa Ana, 54
Santo Niño, 65
Sarawak Dayak, 84
Saya, 51
Sayfoedin, 117
Schilderijen, 106, 108, 109, 114
Schilderijtjes, 108
'*Sepah*' (chewed betel nut), 95
Seventeenth century, 8, 18, 23, 24, 28, 30, 32, 83, 87–91, 93, 94, 104, 114–116
Shawl collars (*pañuelo*), 51
Shaykh Yusuf al-Makassari, 95
Sherbet, 87
Sierra Madre, 55
Silver, 3, 6, 16, 17, 21, 22, 49, 88, 112
Sim Tjimko, 114
Sinamay, soft, fine cloth, 51, 53
Sino-Filipino-Muslim trade networks, 48
Sixteenth century, 5, 17, 33, 69, 76, 82
Skeletons, 77
Social ladder, 118
Social practices, 11, 76
Souchong, 89
South China, 77
Southeast Asia, 6, 7, 11, 13, 16, 20–24, 26, 31, 32, 36, 56, 58, 68, 76–79, 82, 83, 86–88, 93, 95, 96
South Pacific, 77
South Sulawesi, 80, 87, 90, 92, 95
Spaniards, 54, 60, 64, 82, 83
Spanish Baroque, 45
Spanish crown, 48, 58, 65, 83
Spanish era, 44
Spices, 3, 9, 48–50, 83, 84
Spice trade, 9, 48

Spirit world, 78
Spitting, 79, 81
Sri Lanka, 12, 91, 93
St. Christopher, 62, 65
St. James, 55
St. James the Moorslayer, 65
'*Strootjes*', 84
St. Tomas de Villanueva, 62
Suarez, Francisco, 60
Sufi, 93
Sugar, 88, 89, 91, 104
Sulawesi, 86
Sulu Sea, 60
Sumatra, 48, 78, 80, 89, 94, 96
Swettenham, Frank, 80, 87

T
Taal, 54, 55, 57
Tabriya, 62
Tagalog, 55
Taiwan, 26, 32, 82, 94, 106
Tambourin necklace, 61
Tamil, 104, 105
Tanay, 55
Taro (*Colocasi esculenta*), 49
Taytay, 55
Tea, 11, 12, 14, 76, 78, 79, 87–94
Tequitqui, 69
Ternate, 60, 90, 117
Tetuan battle, 65
Thailand, 3, 7, 21–23, 32, 48, 77, 79, 81, 83, 84, 87–89, 91, 95
Theobromine, 76
Theravada Buddhism, 93
Theravada Buddhist monks, 95
Thitsi, 23–25
Tibetan Buddhist monasteries, 95
Tigbauan church, 61, 62, 67
Tobacco, 11, 46, 50, 60, 76, 82–87, 92, 94–97
Tocino del cielo, 57

Tondo, 4, 54
Toxicodendron vernicifluum, 22
Trans-Pacific, 7, 49, 50
Trans-Pacific trade, 49
Tuanku Nan Rinceh, 94
Tuberculosis, 79
Tumauini, 46
Twentieth century, 11, 80, 85, 87, 94

U
Ube (*Dioscorea hispida*), 49
Upper middle classes, 118
Urushi, 17, 22, 24

V
Vandalas (forced sales), 58
Van Dam, Pieter, 108
Vanilla, 50
Vasos sagrados, 60
Vietnam, 23, 82, 83, 88, 93, 95
Vinant, Gillis, 106, 108
Virginia tobacco, 85, 86
Virgin of Caysasay, 56
Visayan Ilonggos, 60
Visayas, 8, 44, 47, 48, 51, 52, 60, 66, 67
Visita, 55

W
Wahhabi of Arabia, 94
Weaving, 47, 51, 61, 68
Western India, 12, 90
Westernization, 8, 81
West Sumatra, 80, 94, 96
Wet markets, 86
Wet-rice cultivation, 55
White teeth, 82
Willem Arnold Alting, 116
Wine, 82, 83, 94, 95, 114

Winstedt, R.O., 80, 86
World War II, 81, 117

Y
Yema, 57
Yemen, 12, 90
Yunnan, 79

Z
Zapote plant, 66
Zhejiang Provinces, 50
Zialcita, Fernando Nakpil, 47, 66